Dale Pinnock

Fakeaways

Dale Pinnock
Fakeaways

Healthy, budget-friendly
takeaways for everyday
home cooking

hamlyn

An Hachette UK Company
www.hachette.co.uk

First published in Great Britain in 2019 by Hamlyn,
a division of Octopus Publishing Group Ltd
Carmelite House
50 Victoria Embankment
London EC4Y 0DZ
www.octopusbooks.co.uk

ISBN 978-0-600-63606-9

A CIP catalogue record for this book is available from the British Library.

Printed and bound in China

10 9 8 7 6 5 4 3 2 1

Editorial Director: Eleanor Maxfield
Senior Editor: Sophie Elletson
Design and Art Direction: Smith & Gilmour
Photography: Faith Mason
Food Styling: Phil Mundy
Props Stylist: Polly Webb-Wilson
Production Manager: Caroline Alberti

INTRODUCTION

Takeaways. We all love them, and I am certainly no exception. They are a great treat, something to have when friends visit or for a special occasion. Generally, getting the odd takeaway is enjoyable and having one now and again doesn't present any kind of problem.

The issue is that so many of us are now reaching for a takeaway over a home-cooked meal most days of the week. A lot of us are even doing this for two or three meals a day. This is when we begin to have a problem. This is where the occasional treat turns into something that can have a profoundly damaging effect on our health. I know this may sound a little dramatic, but as you will soon see, the danger is very real when we consume takeaways to this extreme level.

Enter *Fakeaways*! This book is full of recipes for your favourite takeaways that you can make at home. All of them are quick and use cheap and accessible ingredients. Once you have your storecupboard ingredients (see page 191) they'll be a complete doddle. My versions are also tonnes healthier – and therefore you can enjoy them regularly! I've done some super-simple swaps, such as substituting regular white pasta for wholegrain, and white rice with brown,

but I've also massively upped the nutrient content as well as drastically cut the sugar and other nasties. Get the kids involved – they'll love making my Pizza with a Punch, Baked Spring Rolls and the Tex-mex Beef Burgers. These really are recipes for the whole family.

But what's the problem with takeaways exactly? It is the cumulative effect of these calorie-dense meals and the undesirable ingredients that begins to cause damage? Let's take a look in more detail at some of the nasties that can be found in your average takeaway.

REFINED AND SIMPLE CARBOHYDRATES

Most of the common takeaways that we are likely to choose on a regular basis will be full of refined and simple carbohydrates, which are essentially sources of sugar. They take little effort to digest and the sugars enter our blood stream very rapidly.

When our blood sugar levels rise, the body responds by releasing the hormone insulin. This hormone then binds to an insulin receptor on our cells and lets cells know there is an influx of sugar available for it to take up and use as an energy source. This causes the cells to open up a doorway known as a glucose transporter so that the sugar can enter the cell. Once the cells have taken in their fair share, any left over will be stored in the liver and skeletal muscles in the form of glycogen, which is an easily accessed stored sugar. All well and good.

The problem we face with large doses of simple carbohydrates is that they deliver more glucose in a single sitting than we are designed to cope with. Our cells get full quickly and close the doors to more glucose entering because an excess of glucose within the cell can cause damage. Then our glycogen stores get full. After a large dose of refined and simple carbs, however, blood sugar will still often be very high even after the two usual mechanisms are saturated. The body still needs to bring blood glucose back into normal range so it sends it to the liver where it is converted into a fatty substance called triacylglycerol or triglycerides. These fatty substances are the second storage means employed by the body and they get stored directly in . . . our fat cells! And we gain weight. This is energy that is squirrelled away for a rainy day. The problem for many of us is that the rainy day never comes.

So, problem number 1 is we put on weight. Problem number 2 is that these fatty substances are sent to the fat cells via our circulation. When in circulation they are susceptible to oxidative damage which then in turn can damage the blood vessel walls and set the stage for heart disease. Problem 3 is that raised triglycerides can in turn cause an elevation of the 'bad' LDL cholesterol. Pretty gruesome stuff.

If this set of events continues then yet another problem arises. If our blood sugar gets too high too often, we end up releasing higher and higher levels of insulin. After a while our cells become less responsive to the insulin signal. Soon we become 'insulin resistant' and this can set the stage for type 2 diabetes.

So what do we need to look out for? White bread, white rice, white pasta, sugary sauces. These are the worst contenders. Think of the high-street pizzas that have a base of stodgy white bread an inch thick. Or the dishes at the popular Asian food outlet that are essentially a box of white rice with a tickle of protein. Cheap pasta dishes. The restaurant sauces that have a sticky or gloopy texture to them such as sweet and sour sauce, sticky wings and the like …they are full of sugar.

Simply avoiding these types of carbohydrates can have a huge impact on your day-to-day health.

REFINED VEGETABLE OILS AND TRANS FATS

The next group of problematic substances that we find in most takeaways are the refined oils and trans fats.

Refined oils include your everyday vegetable oil, sunflower oil, corn oil, soy bean oil and the like. We are not talking about olive oil here. We are talking the cheap bulk oils, and also ironically the oils we were told were better for our hearts in comparison to saturated fats. But why are these such an issue? Well, it is all down to the fatty acids they contain. Fatty acids are a group of fats that are biologically active and absolutely vital to our health and the health of every single cell in the body. They are called essential because we have to get them from our diet. Our body cannot manufacture them.

There are two types of essential fatty acids – omega 3 and omega 6. These fatty acids play such a vast and varied role in human physiology, it is really rather mind-blowing. They are involved in maintaining the structure of cell membranes, the myelin sheath (a specialized fatty coating on the outside of nerve cells), and even the eyes. They are also metabolic building blocks that the body uses to create several important substances, one of the most important being a group of communication compounds called prostaglandins, that regulate things like the pain response and inflammation. It is the impact on inflammation that we are going to focus on here, as the effect on health can be profound.

There are three types of prostaglandin – Series 1, Series 2, and Series 3. Series 1 and Series 3 prostaglandins reduce inflammation and tone down the inflammatory response. Series 2 on the other hand switch on and ramp up inflammation. Different fatty acids give rise to different prostaglandins. Remember that as we go through.

So why does this even matter? Well, inflammation is a very, very important reaction in the body and is necessary to our defences – fighting infection and assisting in the repair of damaged tissue. So no inflammation = big problems. However, inflammation that goes beyond a level that is helpful can start to cause untold damage. So keeping inflammation at a healthy level is key. Fatty acid intake can influence this for the better or the worse.

We are reliant on getting omega 3 and omega 6 from our diet. They are essential and we cannot manufacture them. The thing is, our intake of these fatty acids cannot just be willy-nilly. We need to ensure we have a balance.

Why do we need this balance? It will influence what prostaglandins and other by-products are produced, and whether long-term problems arise. If we consume too much of one type, then we can unleash a whole world of problems upon our physiology. The group I am referring to are the omega 6-fatty acids. This group of essential fatty acids are indeed vital to the body. Omega 6-fatty acids are used for normal brain function, growth, and development. However, we only need a very VERY small amount of these per day in order to achieve their physiological goals. Once we go past this level, these fatty acids get shuttled down a different metabolic pathway and are turned into Series 2 prostaglandins – the type that switch on and exacerbate inflammation.

The problem is, omega-6 fatty acids are found naturally in many foods. Our intake has shot through the roof in the last three decades, as we were encouraged to ditch saturated fats and instead opt for 'heart healthy' vegetable oils. Which, it turned out, are composed in such a way that their fatty acid profile is predominantly omega 6.

Omega-3 fatty acids on the other hand have a positive influence on inflammation. The omega-3 fatty acids EPA and DHA are fed into metabolic pathways that produce the anti-inflammatory Series 1 and Series 3 prostaglandins.

It doesn't take a genius to work out that more omega 3 and less omega 6 can begin to have a positive impact on inflammation.

So why does any of this even matter? Well, inflammation that gets out of control, or becomes chronic (i.e. continual for long periods of time) can create serious problems and increase our susceptibility to certain diseases. These include heart disease, inflammatory joint diseases, raised cancer risk, immune dysfunction and many more.

Trans Fats

Trans fats have been in the press a great deal over the last few years and as a result have been banned from many commercially available foods that you would find in your supermarket. However, they do still lurk in ingredients that are used in many takeaways, unless the establishment has specifically made a commitment to get rid of them. Trans fats are fats that have been chemically treated in order to change the way in which they look and feel, and also to help enhance the shelf life of products. These treated fats have been shown to elevate 'bad' LDL cholesterol, lower 'good' HDL and notably increase heart disease risk, to the extent where many countries have banned them all together.

MSG

MSG or monosodium glutamate is a flavour enhancer that is commonly added to Chinese food, canned vegetables, soups and processed meats. It has been used as a food additive for decades. Over the years, there have been many reports of adverse reactions to foods containing MSG. These reactions include:

Headache
Flushing
Sweating
Facial pressure or tightness
Numbness, tingling or burning
    in the face, neck and other areas
Heart palpitations
Chest pain
Nausea
Weakness

In fact, the term 'Chinese restaurant syndrome' has been used to describe the series of symptoms that can occur following the consumption of a meal rich in MSG. These symptoms include a burning sensation at the back of the neck, blistering on both arms, weakness, fatigue and palpitations.

More seriously, MSG has been linked with obesity and metabolic disorders, and it has been suggested that it has detrimental effects on the reproductive organs and brain.

However, some still claim that MSG is perfectly harmless, and to be honest the jury is out. But I think it's best to avoid it as much as possible.

UNDER THE MICROSCOPE

So, before we dive into the amazing homemade delights that you can create in place of your everyday takeaway, let's take a closer look at some of the popular options in a little more detail in terms of their nutritional info. These aren't character assassinations; they are directly from the company's own websites.

Fried Chicken – Thigh

Let's start with a popular fried chicken chain. I have opted for one of the most popular pieces, the thigh, which along with the drumsticks, are the big sellers. So, per thigh we are looking at:

Kcal: 285
Fat: 19.4g
Sat Fat: 4.1g

Get a couple of these down you and you have already clocked up way over 500kcal. I'm not overly concerned with calories if I am honest, as they don't give us the full story. What worries me is the fat picture. Again, I'm no fat-dodger, that's for sure, but look at the total amount of fat, and the low proportion of saturated fat. What does that tell you? The remaining fat will be a refined oil – vegetable oil or sunflower, for example. As we have seen above, these create some big problems and throw our fatty-acid ratios out the window if we aren't careful.

Double Cheese Burger

Let's take a look at a burger from the most popular takeaway outlet on the planet.

Kcal: 508
Fat: 25g
Sat Fat: 9.5g

Again, we see that this is quite a calorie hit for such a small item. And again the biggest concern is the clear difference between the total fat value and the saturated fat value, meaning there are high levels of the refined seed oils/vegetable oil that we really do need to be cutting down on.

Pizza – Pepperoni

Now for a final shocker. Pizza. Pizza can really be the good, the bad and the ugly. The homemade pizza in this book is a long way from many of the high-street versions. The info below is per large pizza. From the many people I have worked with over the years, it is virtually unknown for someone to just have a slice! Most will get a pizza to themselves so I want to open your eyes to what this could mean.

Kcal: 2190
Carbs: 222g
Fat: 95g
Sat Fat: 38g

This is quite a terrifying picture. This amount of carbohydrates coming from refined white flour is in itself hideous. That will push blood sugar through the roof to the extent that many of those events described earlier will take place – elevated triglycerides and insulin. Combine this with a whopping 57g of polyunsaturated fats that will mostly be omega 6, and you have quite the inflammatory load on your hands.

With these above illustrations in mind I don't want to preach to you. That's not what this is about. But if you have found yourself in the position that many are in, where takeaways are dominating your diet, then this is what you are fuelling your body with. This absolutely WILL have severe detrimental effects upon your health in the long term.

Takeaways are great for a treat. I love a good curry or some salt and pepper squid from my local Chinese. But takeaways need to be just that: the occasional treat.

HUGE SAVINGS

Not only are home-cooked versions of your favourite takaways much healthier, they're also much cheaper. Check out the price comparisons below. If you're currently having a takeaway a few times a week, or even a few times a month, these savings will quickly rack up.

Indian
Average cost of takeaway
Tikka Masala for 4 = £19.60
Average cost of fakeaway
Tikka Masala for 4 = £7.83

Chinese
Average cost of takeaway
Duck Pancakes for 4 = £24
Average cost of fakeaway
Roasted Duck Breast with
    Ginger Greens for 4 = £8.89

Italian
Average cost of takeaway
Pizza for 4 = £24.99
Average cost of fakeaway
Pizza with a Punch for 4 = £7.18

Japanese
Average cost of takeaway
Miso Ramen for 2 = £19.70
Average cost of fakeaway
Miso Ramen for 2 = £4.60

Middle Eastern
Average cost of takeaway
Chicken Shish for 1 = £6
Average cost of fakeaway
Chicken Shish Pitta with Goat's
    Cheese and Yogurt Dressing for 1 = £4.70

Thai
Average cost of takeaway
King Prawn Red Curry for 2 = £15.90
Average cost of fakeaway
King Prawn Red Curry for 2 = £10.36

Grills
Average cost of takeaway
Tex-mex Beef Burgers for 2 = £14.80
Average cost of fakeaway
Tex-mex Beef Burgers for 2 = £3.40

CHAPTER ONE
Indian

I have to admit that Indian food is perhaps my favourite food on the planet. With such a high proportion of this country being vegetarian, there are some incredibly healthy dishes that have become classics. Think of a lovely tarka dhal, or a dansak. Or maybe a spicy vegetable-filled dosa. There are some wonderful dishes, and with a bit of tweaking here and there you can make your own versions at home that taste amazing, give you that treat vibe and tick the health boxes too.

These dishes maximize the naturally healthy ingredients that are abundant in Indian cuisine, such as pulses, whole grains and vegetables. What we are dodging here are some of the monstrosities that have made their way into our Indian takeaways – sugar, nasty fats, excessive use of cream, etc. These are your takeaway favourites tidied up for the better.

SERVES: 4
PREP: 5 MINS
COOK: 30 MINS

OK, so chicken tikka masala was invented in the UK, but there's no way I could do a chapter on Indian fakeaways and not include it seeing as it's the most ordered dish from Indian takeaways in the UK. This one is a doddle to make.

TOP MARKS TIKKA MASALA

1 large red onion,
   finely chopped
4 garlic cloves,
   finely chopped
1 cinnamon stick
1 star anise
olive oil, for sautéing
100g tikka masala paste
400g tomato passata
400ml can coconut milk
4 chicken breasts, diced
salt

Sauté the onion, garlic, cinnamon and star anise in a little olive oil, along with a good pinch of salt, for about 8 minutes until the onion has softened and the spices are aromatic.

Add the tikka masala paste and sauté for another 2 minutes.

Add the passata and coconut milk, reserving a few tablespoons to garnish, along with the diced chicken and simmer for 20 minutes, stirring regularly. After 20 minutes or so the sauce should have thickened and the flavours intensified.

Serve with Power Pilau (page 34) and the reserved coconut milk.

Here is one of those vegetarian Indian classics that can make a healthy main dish, or be a nutritious side dish. Plus it's super easy to make!

SAAG ALOO

1 large onion, finely chopped
4 garlic cloves, chopped
1 hot chilli, finely chopped
5cm piece of ginger, peeled and finely chopped
olive oil, for sautéing
1½ teaspoons ground turmeric
½ teaspoon medium chilli powder
750g potatoes, skin left on, diced small
750g spinach, roughly chopped
salt

Sauté the onion, garlic, chilli and ginger in a little olive oil, along with a good pinch of salt.

Stir in the turmeric and chilli powder and sauté for another 5 minutes.

Add the potatoes and a tablespoon of water, stir well, cover and cook for 15–20 minutes.

Add the spinach and cook for another 20 or so minutes, stirring often to avoid sticking. The potatoes should be soft and the mix quite dry.

I absolutely adore this stuff. Tarka dhal is just heavenly. I can have this on its own with a chapati and be perfectly happy. It's packed with B vitamins, plant-based protein, fibre – the works. Again, this can be a healthy side, or a main served up in a bowl with a nice wholemeal bread of some kind or another.

SERVES: 4
PREP: 10 MINS
COOK: 1 HOUR

TARKA DHAL

500g yellow split peas
olive oil, for sautéing
2 tablespoons cumin seeds
1 large onion, finely chopped
2 fresh green chillies,
    finely chopped
5cm piece of ginger, peeled
    and finely chopped
5 large garlic cloves,
    finely chopped
5 tomatoes, roughly chopped
1½ teaspoons ground
    turmeric
1½ teaspoons garam masala
2 teaspoons ground coriander
170ml water
salt

Place the split peas in a pan and cover with water. Bring to the boil and simmer for 40–50 minutes – they should be holding their shape still but soft enough to eat.

Meanwhile, in a frying pan sauté the cumin seeds in a little olive oil for 20–30 seconds, until the fragrance hits you. Add the onions, chillies and ginger plus a good pinch of salt and sauté for about 8 minutes until the onion has softened and has turned golden brown.

Put this onion mix into a food processor along with the tomatoes, and purée. Return this purée to the pan.

Add the ground spices plus the water and simmer for 15–20 minutes.

When the split peas are done, drain and partially break them down with a fork so some are smashed up and others are whole. Add to the frying pan, stir well and add more water if necessary. Simmer for another 5–6 minutes. Taste and add more seasoning if required.

This is a dish that is traditionally made with lamb, but lamb is an ingredient I just don't and won't cook with so I've flipped this into a chicken version, which tastes amazing.

CHICKEN ROGAN JOSH

olive oil, for sautéing
1 large onion, finely chopped
4 garlic cloves, finely chopped
5cm piece of ginger, peeled
   and finely chopped
1 cinnamon stick, broken
   in half
5–6 cardamom pods
½ teaspoon chilli flakes
2 teaspoons cumin seeds
2 teaspoons ground coriander
2 teaspoons garam masala
800g chicken breast, diced
400g can chopped tomatoes
salt
green salad and pitta breads,
   to serve

Sauté the onion, garlic, ginger, cinnamon stick and cardamom pods in a little olive oil with a good pinch of salt until the onion has softened.

Add the remaining spices and cook for another minute or two until the spices start to stick to the bottom of the pan.

Add the chicken and stir well to coat in the spices. Cook for another 2–3 minutes, stirring frequently.

Add the chopped tomatoes and simmer for 20 minutes, stirring often.

Serve with a green salad and some warmed pitta breads.

This vivid-green beauty packs a nice nutritional punch, being particularly high in magnesium from all the spinach used in the base. Paneer is an Indian firm cheese that is now available in almost all supermarkets.

PALAK PANEER

olive oil, for sautéing
½ teaspoon cumin seeds
1 large onion, finely chopped
4 garlic cloves, finely chopped
1 medium tomato, finely chopped
½ teaspoon ground turmeric
½ teaspoon chilli powder
½ teaspoon garam masala
250g paneer (tofu can be used as an alternative), cubed
2 tablespoons coconut cream
salt

For the spinach purée:
250g fresh spinach
1 green chilli, chopped
2.5cm piece of ginger, peeled and roughly chopped
1 garlic clove, roughly chopped

Nutritional nugget

Spinach is one of the highest sources of magnesium, meaning this dish is packed with it. We need magnesium for energy and a healthy nervous system but it is important for a huge number of processes in the body. Paneer is a great source of protein, especially for vegetarians.

To make the spinach purée, drop the spinach into a pan of freshly boiled water, then immediately take the pan off the heat. Leave in the water for 1 minute, so it has time to gently wilt.

Drain the spinach and let it steam-dry for 30 seconds or so. Once it has dried, place it into a food processor along with the green chilli, ginger and garlic. Blitz into a smooth, vivid green-purée.

Put a small amount of olive oil into a pan and place on a high heat. Once the oil is hot, add the cumin seeds and allow them to crackle. Add the onion and a good pinch of salt and sauté.

Add the garlic and sauté for another 2–3 minutes.

Add the chopped tomato and continue to cook for 5 minutes until it softens and has begun to reduce down. At this stage, add the turmeric and chilli powder. Cook for another 2–3 minutes.

Add the spinach purée, plus around 100ml of water. Simmer for 8–10 minutes until the vividness of the green from the spinach has dulled and the sauce has thickened.

Add the garam masala and the paneer and mix well. Simmer for a minute or so. Finally, add the coconut cream.

It's pretty hard to go wrong with this healthy staple of Indian cuisine. Some of the takeaway versions, however, are such a bright fluorescent red, you have to question what on earth has gone into them. Sugar is often added too, so something that should be lean protein can instead end up packed with empty calories and additives.

SERVES: 4
PREP: 15 MINS PLUS
MARINATING TIME
COOK: 30 MINS

TANDOORI CHICKEN

8 chicken thighs, on the bone

For the marinade:
150ml Greek yogurt
5cm piece of ginger,
    peeled and grated
4 garlic cloves,
    very finely chopped
½ teaspoon garam masala
½ teaspoon cumin
½ teaspoon turmeric
½ teaspoon chilli powder
salt

Mix all the marinade ingredients together and season with a little salt. Stir well.

Place the chicken in a dish. Make some deep cuts into the flesh and pour over the marinade. Leave for at least an hour to marinate, but for best results, leave overnight.

Preheat the oven to 180°C, 160°C Fan, Gas Mark 4. Remove the chicken from the dish and place gently in a baking tray, being careful not to dislodge too much marinade as you do.

Bake in the oven for 25–30 minutes.

Serve with a salad and a vegetable side such as Saag Aloo (page 18) or Tarka Dhal (page 21).

This beautiful chickpea curry is great as both a main course and a side. Chickpeas are high in fibre, B vitamins, iron and zinc.

CHANA MASALA

4 garlic cloves, chopped
1 large onion,
    roughly chopped
2.5cm piece of ginger,
    peeled and finely chopped
olive oil, for sautéing
400g can chopped tomatoes
1 tablespoon tahini
½ tablespoon garam masala
½ tablespoon ground
    turmeric
½ tablespoon ground cumin
400g can chickpeas,
    drained and rinsed
juice of ¼ of a lemon
100g baby spinach
salt

Put the garlic, onions and ginger into a food processor and blitz into a paste.

Heat a little olive oil in a pan over a medium heat. Transfer the paste to the pan and sauté it, along with a good pinch of salt, for around 8 minutes or so. I use the general rule of thumb that if you think it's done, give it another 3 minutes. You really want to mellow the flavour.

Add the chopped tomatoes, tahini and spices and simmer for around 10 minutes.

Add the chickpeas and simmer for a further 10 minutes. Finally, add the lemon juice.

You can jazz it up and give the nutrients a boost by throwing in some baby spinach for the last minute or so of cooking.

Nutritional nugget

This dish is full of anti-inflammatory spices. The chickpeas contain numerous vitamins and minerals, including B vitamins, iron and zinc. The addition of spinach here also gives a nutritional boost, as it contains magnesium, iron and calcium, vitamins K and A, and folate (B9).

This is my absolute favourite curry when I go out to an Indian restaurant. Actually, I use it as the benchmark for how good the restaurant is. If their dansak is on point, then I will be a regular. However, one of the problems with a restaurant dansak is that it can contain a lot of sugar. This version allows you to control what goes into it.

SERVES: 4
PREP: 10 MINS
COOK: 45 MINS

VEGETABLE DANSAK

100g red lentils
400g can chopped tomatoes
1 teaspoon ground turmeric
olive oil, for sautéing
1 large red onion,
    roughly chopped
4 garlic cloves, finely chopped
2.5cm piece of ginger,
    peeled and grated
1 red chilli, finely sliced
4 cardamom pods, squashed
200g mushrooms, sliced
200g courgettes, sliced
    into half circles
2 teaspoons ground cumin
1 teaspoon ground coriander
100g baby spinach
salt

Put the lentils and tomatoes into a pan with the turmeric, then add water to cover everything by about 2cm. Place the pan over a medium heat and simmer gently for 20 mins until the lentils have softened.

Meanwhile, in a separate pan, sauté the onions, garlic, ginger, chilli and cardamom in a little olive oil, along with a pinch of salt, for about 8 minutes until the onion has softened.

Add the mushrooms and courgettes plus the ground cumin and coriander and sauté for another 3–4 minutes.

When the lentils are done, add them to the pan with the onion mix, plus about 200ml of water, then simmer for 15–20 minutes.

Add the baby spinach and stir until it has wilted.

Serve with Power Pilau (page 34).

Nutritional nugget

This is chock full of nutrients from all the veg, herbs and spices. Mushrooms contain a polysaccharide (a type of sugar) called beta-glucan which has been shown to be both anti-inflammatory and to boost immunity, especially in the gut.

This classic side dish is great with Chana Masala (page 28) and some cooked spinach. Simple, flavoursome and light.

BOMBAY POTATOES

olive oil, for sautéing
½ red onion, finely chopped
2 garlic cloves, finely chopped
½ small green chilli,
   finely sliced
½ teaspoon mustard seeds
½ teaspoon ground turmeric
350g potatoes, skins left on,
   chopped

Bring a pan of salted water to the boil. Add the chopped potatoes and boil for 10 minutes, or until just tender. Drain and set aside.

In a pan over a medium heat, sauté the onions, garlic, chilli and mustard seeds in a little olive oil, along with a pinch of salt, for about 8 minutes until the onions have softened.

Add the turmeric and mix well. Add the potatoes to the mix and stir well to coat them. Cook for around 6–8 minutes, stirring occasionally, until the potatoes get slightly crispy edges.

Cover and cook for another 5 minutes.

This makes a great accompaniment to all of the Indian dishes here. This recipe uses brown basmati rice and is jewelled with different goodies to give a nutritional boost. It's packed with B vitamins, fibre and magnesium. One thing I really want you to do is to avoid processed carbohydrates like white bread, white rice, white pasta, etc. Instead I want you to swap permanently over to the whole grains.

POWER PILAU

100g brown basmati rice
olive oil, for sautéing
½ red onion, finely chopped
½ courgette, finely chopped
½ teaspoon ground turmeric
1 tablespoon goji berries
15g fresh coriander,
   roughly torn

Nutritional nugget

Using brown rice instead of white rice here means this dish is packed with B vitamins and fibre. B vitamins are essential or energy production and the fibre slows down digestion, meaning your blood sugar levels – and therefore energy levels – stay nice and even.

Place the rice in a pan over a medium heat, cover with water from a freshly boiled kettle and bring to the boil. Turn down the heat to low and simmer for 20–30 minutes until the rice is soft.

While the rice is cooking, heat a little olive oil in a pan and sauté the onions and courgette for about 8 minutes until they are both soft.

Drain the rice and add it to the sautéed veg. Add the turmeric and goji berries and mix everything together well until the rice has taken on the yellow colour of the turmeric.

Add the coriander and stir it through the rice.

CHAPTER TWO
Chinese

This is undoubtedly one of the most popular takeaway options in the UK. However, it's also where we see some of the worst-quality takeaways. Added sugar, monosodium glutamate, cheap oils and dishes that don't even come close to their original incarnations are all too common.

I've spent a lot of time in Hong Kong and in Chinese communities in Malaysia and have seen that this cuisine can represent some incredibly healthy food when done right. It's such a shame that outside of Chinatown or certain high-end Chinese restaurants, this is a takeaway option that has really lost its way.

My versions aim to bring the best of these favourite dishes and healthy cooking principles together to create a far more appealing offering!

OK, let's start this thing nice and simply. We'll begin with a pimped-up version of one of the staple Chinese takeaway side dishes. This is a pretty basic recipe but makes a perfect filling and nutrient-dense alternative.

EGG & VEGETABLE FRIED RICE

120g brown rice
olive oil, for sautéing
2 garlic cloves, finely chopped
1 red onion, finely chopped
2 spring onions,
    finely chopped
4 tablespoons frozen peas
2 teaspoons soy sauce
2 large eggs

Put the rice into a saucepan and cover with boiling water. Simmer for 20–25 minutes until cooked. Drain and set aside.

In a frying pan, sauté the garlic, red onions and spring onions in a little olive oil over a medium heat for about 8 minutes until the onions have softened.

Add the peas and sauté for another 3–5 minutes until the peas are cooked.

Add the rice and mix everything together thoroughly. Add the soy sauce and mix well again.

In a separate pan, crack in the eggs and whisk together over a high heat to make what is essentially scrambled egg. Transfer the cooked egg to the rice mixture and stir through until thoroughly mixed in with everything else.

SERVES: 2
PREP: 10 MINS
COOK: 15 MINS

This is a super-easy favourite to recreate and one that I do at home quite often when I don't feel like making anything extravagant for dinner. There is definitely something comforting about noodles.

VEGETABLE CHOW MEIN

100g egg noodles
olive oil, for sautéing
1 large red onion,
    halved and sliced
3 garlic cloves,
    finely chopped
2 large spring onions,
    cut into batons
150g chestnut mushrooms,
    sliced
2 handfuls of baby spinach
2 tablespoons soy sauce
2 teaspoons toasted
    sesame oil
salt (optional)

Place the noodles in a saucepan, cover with boiling water and cook according to the packet instructions. Drain and set aside.

In a frying pan, sauté the red onion, garlic and spring onions in a little olive oil over a medium heat for about 8 minutes until the onion softens.

Add the mushrooms and continue to sauté for another 4–5 minutes.

Add the spinach and sauté just long enough to wilt it.

Add the cooked noodles and mix all the ingredients together.

Finally, add the soy sauce and sesame oil and mix well.

Season with a little salt if desired before serving.

This is another of those takeaway favourites that really doesn't need to be the sugar bomb that it often is. A few of the staple Chinese-flavour sauces blended together and it's job done. This dish can work great with tofu and chicken too.

SERVES: 2
PREP: 5 MINS
COOK: 12 MINS

KING PRAWNS WITH CASHEW NUTS

olive oil, for sautéing
4 garlic cloves,
    finely chopped
1 large red onion, sliced
250g raw shelled king prawns
70g cashew nuts
2 tablespoons soy sauce
3 teaspoons rice wine vinegar
2 teaspoons toasted
    sesame oil
spring onion, finely sliced,
    to garnish

In a pan, sauté the onion and garlic in a little olive oil over a medium heat for about 8 minutes until the onion has softened.

Add the king prawns, cashew nuts and the liquid ingredients and simmer for 5–7 minutes until the prawns are cooked.

Garnish with the spring onion. Serve with plain brown rice or Egg and Vegetable Fried Rice (page 38)

This is a lovely dish that is very easy to make. The typical takeaway version is laden with fat and sugar. This version is nice and lean, and leaves out the spoonfuls of sugar that are commonly added.

MA PO TOFU

olive oil, for sautéing
1 red onion, finely chopped
2cm piece of ginger, peeled
   and finely chopped
1 spring onion, sliced
4 garlic cloves, finely chopped
1 teaspoon chilli bean sauce
100g minced chicken breast
250g soft tofu, cubed
50ml chicken stock
2 teaspoons soy sauce
2 teaspoons rice wine vinegar
salt
steamed spring greens,
   to serve

In a pan, sauté the onion, ginger, spring onion and garlic in a little olive oil, with a good pinch of salt, over a medium heat for about 8 minutes until the red onion has softened. Add the chilli bean paste and stir well.

Add the minced chicken and sauté for 6–8 minutes, until the mince is fully cooked.

Add the tofu, chicken stock, soy sauce and rice wine vinegar and simmer for 3–4 minutes.

Serve with the steamed greens.

Nutritional nugget

Tofu is a wonderful source of lean vegan protein. Sulphur-containing compounds in the spring onions, red onions and garlic have been shown to be beneficial for a wide variety of systems in the body, including our cardiovascular system, immune system, digestive system, endocrine system, and for detoxification.

This dish can be one of the absolute worst things you will find at a Chinese takeaway. That tub of sticky fluorescent-orange gloop that is basically pure sugar and colouring with an MSG chaser is hideously bad for you. Yet looking at traditional recipes, it can be completely divine. This recipe gets back to basics, packs a good amount of flavour and is full of nutrients.

SERVES: 2
PREP: 10 MINS
COOK: 20 MINS

SWEET & SOUR CHICKEN

olive oil, for sautéing
1 large red onion, halved
    and cut into slices
3 garlic cloves, finely chopped
1 red pepper, deseeded and
    cut into 2cm chunks
1 green pepper, deseeded
    and cut into 2cm chunks
2 chicken breasts, sliced
2 tablespoons honey
2 tablespoons pineapple juice
1 tablespoon passata
3 teaspoons cider vinegar
brown rice, to serve

In a pan, sauté the onions, garlic and peppers in a little olive oil over a medium heat for about 8 minutes until the peppers and onions have softened.

Add the chicken and sauté for another 8 minutes or so.

Add the honey, pineapple juice, passata and cider vinegar. Simmer for another 6–7 minutes until the sauce thickens a little and the chicken is cooked through.

Serve with steamed brown rice.

This is an absolutely delicious dish that is incredibly moreish and is sure to become a family favourite.

ROASTED DUCK BREAST WITH GARLIC GINGER GREENS

1 tablespoon honey
2 teaspoons soy sauce
2 teaspoons toasted
    sesame oil
2 teaspoons Chinese
    five-spice powder
2 duck breasts
1 tablespoon sesame
    seeds, toasted

For the greens:
olive oil, for sautéing
handful of shredded
    spring greens
handful of curly kale
handful of spinach
3 garlic cloves, finely chopped
2cm piece of ginger,
    peeled and finely chopped

Preheat the oven to 200°C, 180°C Fan, Gas Mark 6.

Mix the honey, soy sauce, toasted sesame oil and five-spice powder together to make a sauce/marinade.

Score the skin of the duck breasts and place them skin-side down in a hot frying pan to sear them and get some crispiness. Then place the breasts skin-side up on a baking tray. Pour two-thirds of the sauce over them and bake in the oven for 20 minutes. At this stage pour the remainder of the sauce over them and cook for another 5 minutes.

While the duck is in the oven, in a pan, sauté the greens in a little olive oil for a few minutes until they are almost wilted. Add the garlic and ginger and sauté for another 3–4 minutes.

Slice the duck breasts into 1cm slices and place on top of the greens. Sprinkle with the toasted sesame seeds.

Nutritional nugget

Duck contains a whole host of vitamins and minerals. It is a good source of B12 (B12 is only found in animal products). This vital B vitamin is essential for our brain and nervous system, and for energy production.

SERVES: 2
PREP: 10 MINS
COOK: 15 MINS

This is a beautifully zingy and flavoursome dish that boosts digestive health and immunity. Winner!

KING PRAWNS WITH GINGER & SPRING ONIONS

olive oil, for sautéing
½ red onion, chopped
3 garlic cloves, finely chopped
4 spring onions,
    cut into batons
5cm piece of ginger, peeled
    and cut into thin slices
170g raw shelled king prawns
2 teaspoons oyster sauce
2 teaspoons soy sauce
dash of rice wine vinegar
50ml water
1 teaspoon corn flour,
    dissolved in 1
    tablespoon water
salt
brown rice, to serve

In a pan, sauté the onion, garlic, spring onions and ginger in a little olive oil, with a pinch of salt, over a medium heat for about 8 minutes until the onion has softened.

Add the king prawns, oyster sauce, soy sauce, rice wine vinegar and water and simmer for 4–5 minutes until the prawns are cooked.

Add the corn flour and water mixture and stir to thicken the sauce.

Serve with steamed brown rice.

Nutritional nugget

Essential oils in the ginger ease bloating and the zinc in the prawns supports white blood cell function.

This is a fantastic nutrient-dense dish.
Quick, tasty and great to eat cold the next day.

BEEF & BROCCOLI IN BLACK BEAN SAUCE

300g broccoli, cut into
   small florets
olive oil, for sautéing
3 garlic cloves, finely chopped
2cm piece of ginger, peeled
   and finely chopped
1 sirloin steak, cut into
   thin strips
2 tablespoons Chinese
   black bean sauce
2 teaspoons rice wine vinegar
1 teaspoon toasted sesame oil
brown rice, to serve

Place the broccoli florets in a saucepan and cover with boiling water. Simmer for a couple of minutes until tender.

In a frying pan, sauté the garlic and ginger in a little olive oil for 2–3 minutes.

Add the beef and stir-fry for 3–4 minutes.

Add the broccoli, black bean sauce, rice wine vinegar and sesame oil and simmer for 3–4 minutes until the sauce has thickened a little and the beef is cooked through.

Serve with steamed brown rice.

Nutritional nugget

This dish is packed with iron and zinc from the beef and vitamin C and magnesium from the broccoli.

A gorgeous, fiery, peppery dish that packs quite a punch. Perfect with some sautéed greens and a bit of brown rice.

KUNG PAO CHICKEN

4 garlic cloves, finely chopped
5cm piece of ginger, peeled and finely chopped
2 spring onions, chopped
3 dried red chillies
2 chicken breasts, diced
1 heaped tablespoon runny honey
2 tablespoons soy sauce
½ tablespoon rice wine vinegar
2 teaspoons ground black pepper
salt
sautéed greens and brown rice, to serve
50g unsalted peanuts, to garnish

In a pan, sauté the garlic, ginger, spring onions and chillies in a little olive oil, with a pinch of salt, over a medium heat for 3–5 minutes.

Add the diced chicken and sauté for 5–7 minutes, until the chicken is cooked through.

Add the honey, soy sauce, rice wine vinegar and black pepper. Simmer for 4 minutes.

Sprinkle the peanuts over as a garnish.

Serve with sautéed greens and brown rice.

I do love a spring roll but 99 per cent of the time they have been deep-fried in oil that is old and been used many times. This type of oil is basically a free-radical soup. These baked versions deliver all of the deliciousness minus the grease. They are great dipped in a bit of sweet chilli sauce or the gorgeous peanut butter sauce below.

BAKED SPRING ROLLS

12 square spring roll wrappers
olive oil, for brushing

*Flavouring for the
vegetable filling:*
5cm piece of ginger,
    peeled and finely grated
1 large garlic clove,
    finely chopped
2 tablespoons dark soy sauce
½ tablespoon toasted sesame oil
2 teaspoons Chinese
    five-spice powder

Vegetable filling:
½ courgette, cut into batons
1 red pepper, deseeded and
    cut into thin strips
1 large carrot, cut into thin strips
wedge of red cabbage,
    shredded
2 small spring onions, white
    part finely sliced, green part
    cut lengthwise into thin strips

Peanut dipping sauce:
1 large garlic clove,
    finely chopped
1 red chilli, finely chopped
1 tablespoon smooth
    peanut butter
2 teaspoons soy sauce
2 teaspoons honey
1½ tablespoons water
½ teaspoon Chinese
    five-spice powder

Preheat oven to 200°C, 180°C Fan, Gas Mark 6.

Mix together the flavouring ingredients and dress the vegetable filling, tossing together well.

Soak a spring roll wrapper in warm water for 10–15 seconds then remove and shake off the excess. Lay the wrapper down on a clean surface with one of the corners pointed towards you. Place a stack of the vegetables along the bottom corner of the wrapper. Take the bottom corner and fold it over the filling. Roll towards the centre of the wrapper.

When you get halfway, fold the left and right sides towards the middle, then continue rolling until you get to the end and the familiar spring roll shape has formed. Repeat for all wrappers.

Place the rolls onto a baking dish lined with greaseproof paper and brush each one with a thin layer of olive oil. Bake for 15 minutes before flipping over and cooking for another 5 minutes.

While the rolls are cooking, combine all the dipping sauce ingredients and mix well to make a smooth satay-style dip. You can add more water if you want a runnier consistency. Serve alongside the spring rolls.

CHAPTER THREE
Italian

Italian food has the potential to be some of the healthiest food in the world. With an abundance of fresh vegetables, fish and seafood, pulses, olive oil and the like, this cuisine is fabulous. Sadly, though, many of the takeaway outlets that offer Italian food really don't do it justice. All too often there's a heavy reliance on refined carbohydrate options and added sugars, while many of the sauces and ingredients are heavily processed with little nutritional value.

These versions get back to using wholesome ingredients without detracting from the original essence of the dish.

SERVES: 4
PREP: 10 MINS
COOK: 1 HOUR

LOW-CARB LASAGNE

2 courgettes, thinly
    sliced longways
1 large aubergine,
    thinly sliced longways
olive oil, for sautéing
1 large red onion,
    finely chopped
3 garlic cloves, finely chopped
400g lean minced beef
200g chestnut mushrooms,
    finely sliced
400g can chopped tomatoes
1 tablespoon tomato purée
1 tablespoon dried
    mixed herbs
170g garlic and herb
    soft cheese
150g grated mozzarella
salt and pepper
green salad, to serve

Nutritional nugget

Using courgettes and aubergines instead of lasagna sheets not only boosts the nutrient content but also helps to keep our blood sugar levels stable by reducing the amount of carbohydrate.

Preheat the oven to 180°C, 160°C Fan, Gas Mark 6. Lay the courgette and aubergine slices on a baking tray, season and place under a grill for 3–4 minutes each side. You may need to do this in batches.

In a pan, sauté the onion and garlic in a little olive oil over a medium heat for about 8 minutes until the onion has softened. Add the minced beef and continue to cook, stirring often, for 4–5 minutes.

Add the sliced mushrooms, chopped tomatoes, tomato purée and mixed herbs, then simmer for 20–25 minutes, stirring regularly. This sounds like a long time, but the extended cooking period gives a beautiful richness to the meat sauce.

In a baking dish, place a layer of courgette and aubergine slices. Top with a layer of the meat sauce. Top the meat sauce with another layer of aubergine and courgette, then follow with another layer of meat sauce. Spoon over all of the soft cheese. Follow with another aubergine and courgette layer, then another layer of the meat sauce. Repeat until everything is used up. Top with the grated mozzarella and bake in the oven for 20 minutes.

Serve with a fresh green salad.

This is my pimped-up version of a family favourite – it has basically had a full facelift! Swapping to wholemeal pasta helps to prevent carb overload, blood-sugar spikes and high levels of insulin release. Adding the lentils to the ragout supports digestion and cardiovascular health, and stabilizes blood sugar.

SERVES: 4
PREP: 5 MINS
COOK: 30 MINS

SPAGHETTI BOLOGNESE

180g red lentils
olive oil, for sautéing
1 large red onion,
    finely chopped
2 garlic cloves,
    finely chopped
1 red pepper, deseeded
    and finely chopped
2 x 400g cans chopped
    tomatoes
500g lean minced beef
300g wholewheat spaghetti
salt
green salad, to serve

Put the lentils into a saucepan, cover them with boiling water and simmer for about 15 minutes until soft, then drain and set aside.

Meanwhile in a frying pan, sauté the onion, garlic and red pepper in a little olive oil, along with a pinch of salt, over a medium heat for about 8 minutes until they have softened.

Add the minced beef and continue to sauté for another 4–5 minutes.

Add the lentils and chopped tomatoes then simmer for 10–15 minutes until the sauce thickens.

Meanwhile, cook the spaghetti according to the packet instructions, then divide between 4 bowls and top with the sauce.

Serve with a fresh green salad.

I absolutely adore this dish. Fiery, tomatoey loveliness. When you make this from scratch, you have ultimate control over it. Many restaurants add sugar and dodgy fats which make this potentially healthy dish anything but. You won't find any of that nonsense here.

PENNE ARRABBIATA

2 tablespoons olive oil,
    plus a little extra to finish
1 teaspoon chilli flakes
2 garlic cloves, finely sliced
400g can good-quality
    chopped tomatoes
300g wholewheat penne
¼ teaspoon red wine vinegar
handful of basil leaves
salt and pepper

Heat the oil in a frying pan over a medium heat and add the chilli flakes. When they begin to darken, stir in the garlic and cook for a couple of minutes just until it colours slightly.

Add the tomatoes and a generous pinch of salt, breaking up the tomatoes with a spoon. Simmer for about 15 minutes.

Towards the end of the cooking time, cook the pasta in plenty of boiling salted water until just al dente, or according to the packet instructions. The sauce should be thick by this time – if it looks too dry, add a splash of the pasta cooking water.

Stir the vinegar into the sauce and season to taste, then drain the pasta and add it to the sauce. Stir until the sauce coats each piece, then divide between 4 bowls, drizzle over a little oil and tear over the basil leaves.

I have enjoyed this many a time in Rome. It's a stunning dish that is packed with good stuff like carotenoids and dietary fibre. The fatty cheese helps us to absorb more easily the many nutrients that this dish contains.

AUBERGINE PARMIGIANA

olive oil, for brushing
2 large aubergines, cut into
    slices about 5mm thick
2 tablespoons olive oil
100g ricotta
100g Parmesan, grated
    (or alternative vegetarian
    hard cheese)
100g mozzarella, sliced
salt and pepper
green salad or steamed
    greens, to serve

For the tomato sauce:
good splash of olive oil
2 garlic cloves, finely chopped
1 red onion, finely chopped
2 x 400g cans chopped
    tomatoes
2 teaspoons dried oregano
125ml red wine

Preheat the oven to 200°C, 180°C Fan, Gas Mark 6.

Brush the aubergine slices with olive oil on both sides to coat. Heat a griddle pan and cook the aubergines for a couple of minutes on both sides until lightly browned. Set aside while you get on with the tomato sauce.

Heat a little olive oil in a large frying pan and fry the garlic and onion over a medium heat for about 8 minutes until the onion has softened. Add the chopped tomatoes, oregano and wine. Simmer for about 15 minutes until the sauce thickens.

Spread a little tomato sauce over the bottom of a medium-sized roasting tin. Add a layer of aubergine slices and then spread another layer of tomato sauce on top.

Spread half the ricotta on top and sprinkle with Parmesan, salt and pepper. Continue to repeat the layers until all the aubergine is used. Finish with a layer of mozzarella slices topped with a final sprinkle of Parmesan. Bake for 25 minutes.

Serve with a crisp green salad or steamed greens.

This is another of my favourites. Deeply flavoursome and comforting.

SPAGHETTI PUTTANESCA

olive oil, for sautéing
5 anchovy fillets, drained
  and finely chopped
3 garlic cloves, finely sliced,
  crushed or grated
1 green chilli, sliced
300g wholewheat spaghetti
400g can chopped tomatoes
150g (drained weight) pitted
  black olives, roughly
  chopped
2 tablespoons small capers,
  well rinsed and drained
salt and pepper
2–3 tablespoons chopped
  fresh parsley, to serve
  (optional)

Nutritional nugget

Anchovies are packed
with heart-healthy omega-3
fatty acids. They also contain
selenium which is essential
for reducing free radicals
in the body.

Put water for the pasta on to boil. You won't need to get started on the sauce until it is pretty well boiling.

Heat some oil in a pan over a medium heat. Add the finely chopped anchovies and cook for about 3 minutes, pressing and pushing with a wooden spoon, until the anchovies have almost 'melted', then add the garlic and chilli and cook for another minute.

Add the spaghetti to the pan of boiling water and cook according to the packet instructions. When it is almost cooked, scoop out a small amount of the pasta water.

Add the tomatoes, olives and capers to the anchovies and cook for about 10 minutes, stirring every now and again until thickened. Taste for seasoning.

When the spaghetti is cooked, drain it and stir it into the sauce, adding a little of the reserved pasta water, if needed, to help amalgamate the sauce.

Sprinkle with the chopped fresh parsley (if using) to serve.

This dish is such a sexy little number. An absolute flavour bomb. Gnocchi is a very popular dish but by using sweet potatoes instead of regular potatoes, we add more vitamins to the mix. Goat's cheese is also easier on digestion than cow's milk for many people.

SWEET POTATO GNOCCHI WITH WALNUT & GOAT'S CHEESE PESTO

2 medium sweet potatoes
1 tablespoon ricotta
1 large egg
300g wholemeal flour,
    plus extra for dusting
1 teaspoon salt

For the pesto:
100g walnuts
60g fresh basil
70g soft goat's cheese
2 garlic cloves,
    finely chopped
2 teaspoons olive oil

Preheat the oven to 200°C, 180°C Fan, Gas Mark 6.

Poke a few holes in the sweet potatoes and bake for 45 minutes or until soft. When cooked, slice them in half, allow to cool, then finely mash or purée them.

In a large bowl, mix together the mashed sweet potatoes, ricotta, egg, flour and salt. Stir the mixture until it's just combined. If the dough seems wet, add a tablespoon of flour at a time, until you can form it into a ball. The dough should be sticky.

Generously flour a clean counter and scrape the dough out onto it. Cut the dough into four equal pieces. Working with one piece at a time, roll into a rope about 2.5cm thick and cut into bite-size pieces. When all the gnocci have been made, set aside.

Put all the pesto ingredients into a food processor, add a splash of cold water, and blitz on a low-ish setting to create a coarse pesto.

Place the gnocchi in a saucepan and cover with boiling water. Boil until they float to the top. Drain and let them steam dry for a few minutes.

Return the gnocchi to the saucepan and place over a medium/high heat. Stir in the pesto and warm through before serving.

I love pizza, but there is no getting away from the fact that the common takeaway options are just expensive cheese on toast, laden with refined carbohydrates, sugar, trans fats and a list of nasties that alone could fill a book. This version gives you an amazing pizza, but a much, much healthier version.

SERVES: 4
PREP: 20 MINS
COOK: 20 MINS

PIZZA WITH A PUNCH

500g pack of ready-mixed
    multigrain/seeded
    wholemeal bread mix
olive oil, for sautéing
3 handfuls of baby spinach
8 tablespoons tomato passata
2 garlic cloves, finely chopped
100g grated mozzarella
75g blue cheese
½ red onion, thinly sliced
4 teaspoons pesto
salt

Preheat the oven to 180°C, 160°C Fan, Gas Mark 6.

Place the bread mix in a bowl and mix with water according to the packet instructions. Knead and then divide the mix in two. Roll out two pizza bases and place on two floured baking sheets. Part-bake the bases for 5–6 minutes until they are firm and almost starting to turn golden at the edges.

Sauté the spinach in a saucepan with a tiny amount of olive oil until wilted.

Top the bases with the passata and garlic then season with a little salt.

Scatter over the grated mozzarella. Dot the spinach around the two bases, then crumble over the blue cheese. Scatter over the red onion and then finish by dotting with the pesto.

Cook in the oven until the cheese is melted and bubbling, about 10 minutes.

This beautiful and simple risotto is super filling, and so much healthier than the typical restaurant variety. Traditionally risottos will have a lot of Parmesan and butter in them. This one ditches both of those to keep it lighter, but you seriously won't miss them.

SERVES: 4
PREP: 10 MINS
COOK: 35 MINS

SLOW-BURN RISOTTO

2 tablespoons olive oil
2 large red onions,
    finely chopped
4 garlic cloves, finely chopped
120g sun-dried tomatoes,
    sliced
500g short-grain brown rice
2 x 400g cans chopped
    tomatoes
2 litres vegetable stock
2 courgettes, sliced
2 red peppers, deseeded
    and diced
salt

Nutritional nugget

Tomatoes contain many phytonutrients and therefore have outstanding antioxidant and anti-inflammatory properties. They are beneficial for heart health and skin health, and the phytonutrient lycopene has been shown to be particularly helpful for prostate health in men.

Put the olive oil into a large saucepan and set over a medium heat. Sauté the onion and garlic with a pinch of salt for about 8 minutes until the onion has softened.

Add the sun-dried tomatoes, rice and canned tomatoes. Simmer for around 10 minutes until the liquid is noticeably reducing, stirring frequently.

At this stage, begin adding the stock a little at a time, stirring often, topping it up when you notice the liquid beginning to reduce. Keep this up until the rice is almost cooked, about 15–20 minutes in total.

Add the courgettes and red peppers, and continue adding the stock until the rice is cooked and the vegetables have softened.

Divide between 4 plates or bowls.

This dish is a hit on menus the world over. It has the potential to be a super-healthy meal. Seafood is rich in zinc, selenium and protein – pretty much a winner. You just have to make sure the rest of the ingredients are up to the same standard.

SEAFOOD LINGUINE

400g wholewheat linguine
    or spaghetti
2 tablespoons olive oil
2 garlic cloves, thinly sliced
½ red chilli, deseeded
    and finely chopped
200ml dry white wine
220g cherry tomatoes,
    halved
200g mixed seafood
    (prawns, squid
    and scallops)
handful of parsley, chopped

Bring a large pan of salted water to the boil and cook the pasta according to the packet instructions.

Meanwhile, heat the oil in a large frying pan over a medium heat. Add the garlic and chilli and cook for 30 seconds–1 minute until just turning golden. Pour in the wine, then leave to bubble until reduced by half.

Stir the tomatoes into the pan and cook for 1–2 minutes to soften. Add the seafood mix and continue to cook for a further 1–2 minutes or until fully heated through.

Drain the cooked pasta, reserving about a cupful of the cooking water. Return the pasta to the empty pan and tip in the seafood mixture.

Add a little of the pasta cooking water to loosen, then toss together until everything is well mixed, adding more water if needed.

Divide between 4 bowls and sprinkle over the parsley before serving.

It's carbonara – ish! I wanted to create a version of this that is lighter and more nutrient dense, yet still brings the gorgeous culinary delights of a traditional carbonara.

TAGLIATELLE CARBONARISH

400g wholewheat tagliatelle
olive oil, for sautéing
3 garlic cloves,
    finely chopped
1 white onion,
    very finely chopped
3–4 slices of smoked ham
    (try to get one without
    nitrates), torn
3 tablespoons soft cheese
150ml vegetable stock
3 handfuls of baby spinach
green salad, to serve

Bring a large pan of salted water to the boil and cook the tagliatelle according to the packet instructions. Drain and set aside.

In a pan, sauté the garlic and onion in a little olive oil for about 8 minutes until the onion has softened.

Add the ham, soft cheese and vegetable stock and simmer to create a thick, creamy sauce.

Throw in the baby spinach and then the cooked tagliatelle.

Mix well before dividing between 4 bowls and serving with a lovely green salad.

CHAPTER FOUR

Japanese

Japanese cuisine is perhaps some of the healthiest food in the world. I have spent a great deal of time in Japan and have come to appreciate the beautiful subtlety of the flavours and how delicate and fresh the food can be. Most people's idea of Japanese food would include sushi and noodles, and yes, these are definitely some of the best dishes that have made it around the world, but there's a lot more to this cuisine. In this chapter we are going to recreate those takeaway staples, with a bit of traditional fare thrown in to broaden your horizons.

I have spent a lot of time in the city of Fukuoka, the birthplace of ramen. The Japanese adore their ramen and in Fukuoka it is serious business – there are some incredible ramen stalls where the food is mind-blowing. From a health point of view, miso ramen is top of the tree.

SERVES: 2
PREP: 15 MINS
COOK: 40 MINS

MISO RAMEN

1 large skinless chicken breast
2 tablespoons miso paste
100g firm tofu, cubed
5–6 shiitake mushrooms
750ml water
125g soba noodles
2 handfuls of mixed
    shredded greens
2 eggs, soft boiled
4 spring onions, sliced,
    to garnish

Nutritional nugget

Miso is such a nutrient-dense ingredient. This fermented soya bean paste is a rich source of many vitamins, minerals and powerful phytochemicals as well as fibre and protein.

Preheat the oven to 180°C, 160°C Fan, Gas Mark 4.

Put the chicken breast onto a baking sheet and bake for 25 minutes.

Put the miso paste, tofu, shiitake and the water into a saucepan and mix well while bringing it up to a gentle simmer.

Place the soba noodles in a second saucepan, cover with boiling water and simmer until soft. Drain and divide between 2 serving bowls.

Add the shredded greens to the serving bowls too.

Cut the chicken into an even number of slices and divide between the two serving bowls.

Pour the miso base over the noodles, greens and chicken in each serving bowl.

Shell the soft-boiled eggs and cut each one in half, placing two halves in each serving bowl. Garnish with the spring onions.

SERVES: 2
PREP: 10 MINS
COOK: 30 MINS

This is now one of the most popular takeaway dishes in the UK, particularly in the south. Most katsu curries from well-known outlets come out at almost 1,000 calories a pop, which is staggering. This one definitely reins that in and gives an extra nutritional bang.

CHICKEN KATSU CURRY

olive oil, for sautéing
   and frying
3 garlic cloves,
   finely chopped
1 large sweet potato,
   peeled and diced
1 tablespoon mild
   curry powder
½ teaspoon Chinese
   five-spice powder
vegetable stock
100g brown rice
2 skinless chicken breasts
70g panko breadcrumbs
3 handfuls of baby spinach
6 radishes, thinly sliced
1 carrot, grated

Put the rice into a pan, cover with boiling water and simmer for about 12 minutes until cooked.

Meanwhile, in a saucepan, sauté the garlic in a little olive oil for a few minutes until it becomes aromatic. Add the diced sweet potato, curry powder and the five-spice powder and enough vegetable stock to cover it by around two-thirds. Place the lid on the pan and simmer until the sweet potato is soft, about 10 minutes.

Put this mixture into a food processor and blend into a smooth sauce.

Using a rolling pin, gently flatten out the chicken breasts. Sprinkle the breadcrumbs onto a tray and drop the chicken breasts in, turning over a couple of times to ensure they are fully coated.

Heat a little olive oil in a pan, carefully add the chicken breasts and pan-fry for 10–12 minutes, turning gently on occasion. You want to ensure the crumbs are crispy and golden brown.

Place the curry sauce back on the heat and reheat gently for a few minutes. At the same time, mix together the baby spinach, radishes and carrot.

Divide the rice between two plates. Cut the chicken into slices about 1cm thick and place next to the rice. Pour over the sauce. Serve with the salad.

SERVES: 4
PREP: 10 MINS
COOK: 15 MINS

CHILLI SQUID

100g plain flour
1 teaspoon chilli powder
1 teaspoon chilli flakes
2 teaspoons salt
500g prepared squid
   cut into rings
olive oil, for deep frying

Dipping sauce:
2 tablespoons soy sauce
3 tablespoons toasted
   sesame oil
3 tablespoons mirin
   (Japanese rice vinegar)
juice of ½ a lime

Preheat the oven to 180°C, 160°C Fan, Gas Mark 4.

Place the flour, chilli powder, chilli flakes and salt into a sandwich bag or freezer bag and mix together well.

Throw the squid rings into the bag of seasoned flour and shake well to ensure that the squid is completely coated.

Fill a wok or saucepan about 3cm deep with olive oil. Heat over a high heat and then drop a piece of bread into it once it starts to bubble. If the bread goes brown in 15 seconds, the oil is ready. Add the squid in batches for about 2 minutes until it starts to get crispy. Remove and then transfer to a greaseproof paper-lined baking tray.

When all the squid has been fried, place the tray in the oven and bake until the squid is golden, about 8–10 minutes.

While the squid is in the oven, mix all the dipping sauce ingredients together and whisk well. Serve alongside the crispy chilli squid.

Go to any of the popular noodle outlets up and down the country and this dish will be one of the most frequently ordered. It's a simple, tasty Japanese, equivalent to a Chinese chow mein.

YAKI SOBA

olive oil, for stir-frying
1 large red onion,
   finely chopped
3 garlic cloves, finely chopped
2cm piece of ginger, peeled
   and sliced into thin batons
2 large spring onions,
   cut into batons
6–7 shiitake mushrooms,
   sliced
120g soba noodles
165g king prawns,
   shells removed
3 handfuls of baby spinach
2 tablespoons
   Worcestershire sauce
1 tablespoon soy sauce
2 tablespoons oyster sauce
2 teaspoons honey
salt

Stir-fry the onion, garlic, ginger and spring onion in a little olive oil, along with a good pinch of sea salt, for about 8 minutes until the onion has softened. Add the sliced mushrooms and stir-fry for another couple of minutes until they start to soften.

Put the noodles into a saucepan, cover with boiling water and simmer for 3–4 minutes until they are soft and separated.

While the noodles are cooking, add the prawns and baby spinach to the onion mix and stir-fry for another 3–4 minutes until the prawns are cooked.

Drain the noodles then add them to the prawn mix. Toss well so that all the ingredients are mixed together well.

Add the Worcestershire sauce, soy sauce, oyster sauce and honey and stir well to coat everything.

This is an incredibly popular dish both here and in Japan. Walk around any Japanese city after dark and you will see food outlets buzzing with suited businessmen, the beer flowing and yakitori skewers being served in their hundreds. The traditional recipe uses refined sugar which I'm swapping out for honey here – still sugar, but less refined so at least you get some minerals with those calories!

CHICKEN YAKITORI

50ml soy sauce
50ml mirin (Japanese rice vinegar)
30ml sake
1 tablespoon honey
200g boneless skinless chicken thighs, cut into bite-size pieces
bamboo skewers
brown rice and stir-fried vegetables, to serve (if having as a main)

Put all the wet ingredients into a bowl and whisk together well.

Add the chicken pieces and toss to ensure they are fully coated.

Hold a skewer above the bowl and thread on 3–4 pieces of chicken, allowing the excess marinade to drip back into the bowl. You will need this later. Repeat until all the chicken is used up.

Heat a griddle pan or a large frying pan over a high heat and lay the skewers in it, then turn the heat down to medium. After a minute or two, turn the skewers and then brush the side that was just cooking with leftover sauce, turn and repeat again. Keep cooking and turning for 10–12 minutes until the chicken is thoroughly cooked and the sauce has gone sticky.

Serve as a snack or as a side. To make into a main meal, serve with brown rice and some stir-fried veggies.

This absolute beauty of a dish was made famous by the high-end Japanese restaurant chain Nobu. I wanted to include this here as it is such a popular dish. Sure, it may not be a takeaway staple but I'm positive that once you get a taste of this, you will become a lifelong fan.

COD WITH MISO SAUCE & GINGERED GREENS

2 tablespoons white
    miso paste
1 tablespoon mirin
    (Japanese rice vinegar)
1 tablespoon light soy sauce
1 teaspoon toasted
    sesame oil
2 cod fillets
olive oil, for stir-frying
2 heads of pak choi,
    separated into
    individual leaves
2cm piece of ginger,
    peeled and grated
salt

Preheat the oven to 180°C, 160°C Fan, Gas Mark 4. Mix the miso, mirin, soy sauce and sesame oil together.

Lay the cod fillets onto a lightly oiled baking tray. Top each fillet with some of the miso sauce but save half of it. Put the tray in the oven and bake for 20 minutes.

While the fish is cooking, begin stir-frying the pak choi in a little olive oil with a small pinch of salt. As it starts to wilt, add the ginger and cook for 3–4 minutes.

Put the leftover miso sauce in neat dollops on two serving plates. Place the cooked cod on top, then pile the pak choi next to the fish.

Nutritional nugget

Pak choi is part of the super-healthy cruciferous family. It contains glucosinolates, sulfur-containing compounds that are great for liver detoxification. Cod is a great source of protein and nutrients such as vitamin B12, iodine and selenium.

This is a type of savoury Japanese pancake. They are absolutely delicious but can be a serious stodge fest as they are cooked with buckets of white flour and often served an inch thick. This version uses wholemeal flour to up the fibre and lots of greens for that veggie hit.

OKONOMIYAKI

100g wholemeal flour
2 eggs, beaten
large handful of curly kale, shredded, thick stalks removed
1 large carrot, grated
1 large leek, thinly sliced
2 tablespoons ground flax seeds
1 teaspoon sesame oil
2 tablespoons soy sauce
1 tablespoon cider vinegar
1 teaspoon honey
2cm piece of fresh ginger, peeled and finely chopped
olive oil, for frying
salt and peper

Put the flour, eggs, kale, carrot, leek and flax seeds together in a large mixing bowl and mix well. You should end up with a bowl of batter-coated vegetables. Season with salt and pepper.

Make a dipping sauce by mixing the sesame oil, soy sauce, cider vinegar, honey and ginger in a bowl, then set aside.

Heat a large frying pan and add a little olive oil, ensuring the base of the pan is coated.

Add half of the the vegetable/batter mixture to the pan. Press down to form a pancake. Cook for 3–4 minutes before carefully turning over. Cook for a further 3–4 minutes, until the whole pancake is crisp and golden. Repeat with the remaining batter.

Slice into wedges and serve with the dipping sauce.

*Donburi - or rice bowls - are a staple in Japan.
I love them in all their guises. This one is super light,
fibre rich, packed with micronutrients and tastes
awesome. Winner!*

VEGAN DONBURI

120g brown rice
olive oil, for sautéing
1 red pepper, deseeded
  and cut into strips
150g shiitake mushrooms,
  sliced
2 handfuls of shredded greens
1 large spring onion, sliced,
  to garnish

For the sauce:
3 tablespoons mirin
  (Japanese rice vinegar)
3 tablespoons soy sauce
1 tablespoon agave nectar
  (or honey)
1 garlic clove, finely chopped
1 teaspoon corn flour

Put the rice into a saucepan and cover with boiling water. Simmer for 40 minutes until soft and fluffy.

Sauté the pepper strips in a little olive oil over a medium heat for about 5 minutes until they begin to soften. Add the shiitake mushrooms and continue to sauté for another 3–4 minutes until they are soft. Add the greens and then all the sauce ingredients and cook for about a minute until the sauce has thickened.

Divide the rice between 2 bowls. Top each with the sticky cooked veg, then garnish each with sliced spring onion.

Nutritional nugget

Peppers are well known for their carotenoid content. Caretenoids are important phytonutrients that have potent antioxidant and anti-inflammatory properties. Peppers are also an excellent source of vitamin C, which is essential for the immune system and indeed all other systems in the body.

This is a gorgeous dish that is really rather moreish. However, the regular version uses blocks of Japanese curry sauce that is generally full of salt, MSG and sugar. Not good. This version is a nod to the original with a nice curry flavour, but without the nasties.

SERVES: 2
PREP: 10 MINS
COOK: 15 MINS

CURRY UDON

120g udon noodles
olive oil, for sautéing
1 large red onion,
    halved then sliced
4 garlic cloves,
    finely chopped
75g shiitake mushrooms,
    sliced
75g cooked king prawns,
    shells removed
2 handfuls of spinach
1 teaspoon medium
    curry powder
2 teaspoons soy sauce
1 teaspoon toasted
    sesame oil
2 large spring onions,
    cut into strips
salt

Put the udon noodles into a saucepan, top with boiling water and simmer until soft. Drain and set aside.

Sauté the red onion and garlic in a little olive oil, along with a good pinch of salt, over a medium heat for about 8 minutes until the onion has softened.

Add the shiitake mushrooms and keep stir-frying for 3–4 minutes until they have softened.

Add the cooked udon noodles, prawns and spinach, then toss well and stir-fry for a minute.

Add the curry powder, soy sauce and sesame oil, then mix together until everything is coated.

Divide between 2 bowls, then garnish with the spring onions before serving.

I know that sushi rolls may look complicated but really they are pretty easy once you get the hang of it. Give these a try. Many takeaway and pre-made sushi rolls are filled with added sugar.

BEGINNERS' SUSHI ROLLS

150g uncooked
    short-grain rice
3 tablespoons mirin
    (Japanese rice vinegar)
1½ teaspoons salt
4 nori seaweed sheets
½ cucumber, peeled,
    cut into small strips
2 tablespoons pickled ginger
1 avocado, peeled, stone
    removed and cut into
    small strips
225g smoked salmon,
    crab meat or tuna, flaked

In a medium saucepan, bring 325ml of water to a boil. Add the rice and stir. Reduce the heat, cover and simmer for 20 minutes.

In a small bowl, mix the mirin and salt. Stir the mixture into the cooked rice. Allow the rice to cool to room temperature.

Preheat the oven to 150°C, 130°C Fan, Gas Mark 2.

On a medium baking tray, heat the nori in the oven for 1–2 minutes, until warm.

Centre one sheet of nori on a bamboo sushi mat. Wet your hands, then use them to spread a quarter of the rice onto the sheet of nori and press it into a thin layer.

Arrange a quarter of the cucumber, ginger, avocado and seafood of your choice in a line down the centre of the rice. Lift the end of the mat and carefully roll it over the ingredients, pressing gently. Keep rolling the mat until the roll is completed, with all the filling enclosed in the nori sheet. Repeat with the remaining ingredients.

Cut each roll into 4–6 slices using a wet, sharp knife. Serve immediately.

CHAPTER FIVE
Middle Eastern

Middle Eastern cuisine can offer a heady mix of flavour, texture and colour. Get it right and it can be some of the healthiest food out there. With lots of pulses, vegetables, fibre and antioxidants, there's plenty of good stuff in the mix. Done badly, however, there can be too many refined carbohydrates and very fatty cuts of meat, which aren't at the best end of the healthy spectrum.

Most of the popular Middle Eastern takeaway options tend to have great lists of small dishes that we can piece together meze-style, which is what I have gone for in this chapter. Many of the mains from such takeaways come with a heap of white rice that could make an army comatose, together with a lame bit of salad. Here we are going to ditch that and create a Middle Eastern meze feast! Think of these recipes as small dishes that you can bring together in any combination for a super-healthy, nutrient-dense treat.

The absolute staple of Middle Eastern cuisine. Falafel may be extremely common but they are also extremely nutritious, filling, fibre rich and delicious.

FALAFEL WITH TAHINI DRESSING

2 x 400g tins chickpeas,
    drained and rinsed
4 garlic cloves, crushed
½ small bunch fresh
    flatleaf parsley
2 teaspoons ground cumin
1 teaspoon ground coriander
1 red onion, very finely
    chopped
2 eggs, lightly beaten
2 tablespoons wholemeal flour
2 tablespoons olive oil,
    plus extra for frying
3 tablespoons tahini
juice of 1 lemon
salt and pepper
coriander leaves, to garnish

Preheat the oven to 200°C, 180° Fan, Gas Mark 6.

Put the chickpeas, half the garlic, the parsley, cumin and coriander in a food processor and whizz to a paste. Transfer to a bowl, add the onion, eggs and flour, then season with salt and pepper and mix well to form a stiff mixture.

Line a baking sheet with baking paper. Shape the falafel mixture into small patties. In batches, shallow-fry the falafels in a little olive oil for 2–3 minutes on each side until starting to turn crispy. Transfer to the baking sheet, then bake in the oven for 10–12 minutes.

Meanwhile, make the dressing by whisking together the 2 tablespoons of olive oil, the tahini, remaining garlic and lemon juice. Garnish the falafel with coriander leaves, then serve with the tahini dressing.

Traditionally koftas are made with lamb. The problem is, lamb isn't the healthiest of meats because of the high fat content, so this light, lean version uses chicken instead.

CHICKEN KOFTAS

1 tablespoon olive oil
1 onion, finely chopped
1 garlic clove, crushed
450g minced chicken
1 bird's-eye chilli, chopped
½ teaspoon ground cinnamon
freshly grated nutmeg,
    to taste
½ teaspoon paprika
½ teaspoon ground cumin
1 tablespoon chopped
    fresh parsley
melted butter and lemon
    juice, to baste
salt and pepper

Preheat the grill to its highest setting.

Heat the oil in a frying pan over a medium heat. Add the onion and garlic and sauté for about 8 minutes until softened. Remove from the heat and allow to cool.

Place the minced chicken into a large bowl. Add the fried onion and garlic mixture.

Add the chilli, cinnamon, nutmeg, paprika, cumin and parsley. Season with salt and pepper and mix together well.

Shape small handfuls of the chicken mixture into walnut-sized balls.

Thread 3 chicken balls onto a skewer (if you're using wooden skewers, soak them in water for 10 minutes beforehand to prevent burning). Repeat with the remaining mixture onto separate skewers, 3 balls to a skewer.

Place the koftas under the grill to cook for 8–10 minutes. Halfway through, turn and baste with butter and lemon juice, then place them back under the grill until cooked through.

Serve with a salad and dips such as Hummus (page 109) and Baba Ganoush (page 110).

I am a self-confessed complete and utter hummus-holic. I love the stuff. Sure, it can be quite calorific, but look where those calories come from: protein, fibre, healthy fats. This divine ambrosia also provides zinc, B vitamins and iron. The recipe here is just a straightforward hummus, but the bowls can be based on falafel (page 102), cooked meats, sautéed vegetables, or a combination of these piled on top of fresh, creamy, delightful hummus… OK, enough of my adoring waffle.

SERVES: 4
PREP: 10 MINS

HUMMUS BOWLS

2 x 400g cans chickpeas
 (1 can drained and rinsed,
 the other with a quarter
 of the liquid retained)
2 garlic cloves, finely chopped
juice of 1½ large lemons
3 tablespoons tahini
2 tablespoons extra-virgin
 olive oil
1 teaspoon sesame seeds
salt, to taste
drizzle of sesame oil,
 to serve

Place all ingredients in a food processor, except the sesame seeds and sesame oil, and blend into a smooth hummus.

Spoon into a bowl, sprinkle over the sesame seeds and drizzle with sesame oil.

Enjoy with some warmed pitta and vegetable crudites, or use as a base for a hummus bowl, as described above.

Nutritional nugget

Chickpeas are full of fibre and have been shown to help lower levels of 'bad' LDL cholesterol. They are also brilliant for blood sugar regulation.

SERVES: 4
PREP: 10 MINS
COOK: 40 MINS

Another absolutely classic dip that is stunning served in a great big dollop alongside cooked meats and roasted vegetables, or just scooped up with a good wholemeal bread like a pitta.

BABA GANOUSH

2 large aubergines
2 tablespoons tahini
2 garlic cloves,
    finely chopped
juice of 1 lemon
2 teaspoons pomegranate
    seeds
small handful of parsley,
    to garnish

Preheat the oven to 200°C, 180° Fan, Gas Mark 6.

Slice the aubergines in half and then score the exposed flesh. Place these scored-side down onto a lightly oiled baking sheet and bake for 35–40 minutes. You want the aubergine to be very, very soft and the skins to be getting a little charred so that a smoky flavour arises.

Allow the aubergine to cool and then transfer to a food processor. Add the tahini, garlic and lemon juice and blitz into a coarse dip.

Spoon into a bowl, top with the pomegranate seeds and garnish with some parsley.

This is a beautiful, filling, flavoursome alternative to the array of weird and wonderful kebabs found on the high street.

CHICKEN SHISH PITTA WITH GOAT'S CHEESE YOGURT DRESSING

1 skinless chicken breast, diced
2 tablespoons goat's cheese
1 tablespoon plain yogurt
juice of ½ a lemon
1 wholemeal pitta bread, warmed
small handful of baby spinach
¼ red onion, finely sliced

For the marinade:
1 tablespoon plain yogurt
½ teaspoon cumin
¼ teaspoon cinnamon
1 teaspoon smoked paprika
2 teaspoons lemon juice
salt and pepper

Preheat the oven to 200°C, 180°C Fan, Gas Mark 6.

Combine the marinade ingredients together in a bowl.

Thread the chicken pieces onto a skewer (if you're using a wooden skewer, soak it in water for 10 minutes beforehand to prevent burning) and place on a baking sheet. Pour the marinade over the chicken and roll the skewer around to ensure all of the chicken is coated. Bake in the oven for 25–30 minutes, turning once.

Combine the goat's cheese, yogurt and lemon juice to make a sauce.

Slice the pitta open, add the spinach and sliced red onion. Remove the chicken from the skewer and add to the pitta, then top with the sauce.

This is a great alternative to plain brown rice. It provides fibre, B vitamins and low-glycaemic carbohydrates. It's a winner all round and is perfect as a side to all of the smaller dishes in this chapter.

MUJADARRA

olive oil, for sautéing
2½ red onions, finely sliced
120g dried green lentils
120g brown rice
½ teaspoon cumin
½ teaspoon cinnamon
salt and pepper

Nutritional nugget

Lentils contain both insoluble and soluble fibre, as well as magnesium and folate, which makes them great for heart health. In fact, they may even help to prevent heart disease.

Put the lentils in a pan and cover them with about 3 times their volume of boiled water. Simmer for about 10 minutes until the lentils have softened.

Add the rice and spices, and continue to simmer for about 20 minutes until the rice has cooked. It may be necessary to top up the water in small amounts but the end product needs to be dry.

Meanwhile, sauté the onions in a little olive oil over a medium heat for 8–10 mintues until they have softened and are starting to brown.

Once the rice has cooked, add in the onions and season with salt and pepper to taste.

This simple, flavoursome stew is a great slow cooker recipe and is also an excellent option for batch cooking as it freezes perfectly.

FASULIA

olive oil, for sautéing
1 large red onion,
    roughly chopped
2 garlic cloves, finely chopped
250g cubed braising steak
400g can chopped tomatoes
2 teaspoons tomato purée
½ teaspoon ground cumin
½ teaspoon ground coriander
½ teaspoon ground cinnamon
200g green beans, topped
    and tailed
chopped coriander leaves,
    to garnish
salt and pepper

Sauté the onion and garlic in a little olive oil until the onion softens.

Add the beef, chopped tomatoes, tomato purée and spices and simmer gently for 1½ hours, stirring occasionally.

Finally, add the green beans and simmer for another 30 minutes. Garnish with chopped coriander leaves before serving.

This dish has become a popular breakfast dish, and you can't seem to go anywhere – in London especially – without seeing it on the brunch menu. But really you can have it any time of day and it's an exceptionally healthy dish. This version, of course, has a twist to give it a nutritional boost.

LIBYAN SHAKSHUKA

olive oil, for sautéing
1 large red onion, halved
    and sliced
3 garlic cloves, finely chopped
1 red pepper, deseeded and
    cut into 1.5cm chunks
400g can chopped tomatoes
1 teaspoon ground cumin
2 teaspoons smoked paprika
4 eggs
100g feta cheese
salt and pepper
chilli flakes, to serve

Nutritional nugget

Eggs contain all of the B vitamins and are one of the highest sources of choline. Choline is an essential nutrient in the production of phosphatidylcholine, one of the most important structural building blocks of a cell. Eggs are also a good source of certain minerals that are difficult to get from other foods, such as selenium and iodine.

Sauté the onion and garlic in a little olive oil over a medium heat for about 8 minutes until the onion has softened.

Add the red pepper and sauté for another 3–4 minutes until it's beginning to soften.

Add the chopped tomatoes, cumin and smoked paprika. Season with salt and pepper to taste.

Simmer for around 20 minutes, stirring frequently, until the sauce thickens and the flavour intensifies.

Once the sauce has thickened, make 4 wells in the sauce. Crack an egg into each well and simmer away until the eggs are cooked. Don't overdo it as you want the yolks to be soft. About 6–8 minutes should suffice.

Crumble over the feta before serving with the chilli flakes.

This is a great sharing plate to have in the centre of the table. It would work just as well as a light main course at half the portion size, served with some Hummus (page 109)… perfect. This platter consists of three items – spiced roasted cauliflower, grilled aubergine and fattoush salad – plus a delicious tahini dressing that goes beautifully over the cauli and aubergine.

SERVES: 4
PREP: 15 MINS
COOK: 30 MINS

VEGGIE PLATTER

Spiced roasted cauliflower:
½ a head of cauliflower
olive oil, for drizzling
½ teaspoon ground cumin
½ teaspoon ground cinnamon
½ teaspoon sumac
salt and pepper to taste
handful of parsley, chopped

Grilled aubergine:
1 large aubergine, cut
    lengthways into slices
    about ½cm thick
olive oil, for drizzling
½ teaspoon cumin
½ teaspoon ground coriander
salt and pepper to taste

Fattoush salad:
200g ripe tomatoes
½ large cucumber
50g radishes
1 spring onion
small bunch of fresh mint
1 stale pitta bread
½ garlic clove, finely chopped
juice of ¼ of a lemon
2 teaspoons cider vinegar
1½ tablespoons olive oil

Tahini dressing:
1 tablespoon tahini
1 garlic clove,
    roughly chopped
juice of 1 lemon
1 tablespoon water

Preheat the oven to 200°C, 180° Fan, Gas Mark 6.

Cut the cauliflower into individual florets and place on a baking tray. Drizzle the cauliflower with a little olive oil. Toss. Sprinkle over the spices and seasoning then toss again. Bake in the oven for 25–30 minutes, stirring occasionally.

Meanwhile, take the aubergine slices and drizzle a little olive oil over them. Sprinkle over the spices and seasoning, then get your hands in and mix everything together to ensure the aubergine is well covered. Leave for about 10 minutes so they start taking on flavour, then place in a hot griddle pan ideally, or a frying pan, and cook for 4 minutes on each side.

For the fattoush salad, cut the tomatoes, cucumber and radish into chunks. Finely chop the spring onion, tear the mint and then combine all of these. Place the pitta bread in the oven for a few minutes, just long enough for it to go crisp and brittle. Combine the garlic, lemon juice, cider vinegar and olive oil to make a dressing. Break the pitta bread into pieces over the salad, then dress.

Combine the tahini dressing ingredients together.

Arrange all of the above dishes onto a platter or place in separate bowls. Dress the cauliflower and the aubergine slices with the tahini dressing. Finally, scatter over the parsley before serving.

CHAPTER SIX

Thai food is one of my absolute favourites.
When visiting the country, I have enjoyed
some real gems – the diversity there is
amazing. From the street vendors to high-
end restaurants, the huge variety of dishes
presented is staggering.

I have to say, though, that many of the
day-to-day Thai takeaways up and down
the UK really don't do this vibrant cuisine
justice and a lot of them are just spicy,
sugary, nondescript dishes that are far from
the original. With these recipes I am aiming
to honour the cuisine at its finest and give
the health-ranking a boost at the same time.

These make a beautiful, flavoursome starter – or you could create larger ones to have with a salad as a main. I recommend getting skinless salmon fillets from the fishmonger as skinning them yourself is very fiddly.

SALMON & PRAWN CAKES

3 skinless salmon fillets
165g raw king prawns,
    shells removed,
    roughly chopped
2 tablespoons Thai red
    curry paste
2 garlic cloves,
    finely chopped
small bunch of fresh
    coriander, roughly
    chopped
olive oil, for pan-frying
salt
sweet chilli sauce, to serve

Place the salmon fillets in a food processor and blitz into a smooth paste. Transfer this to a bowl.

Add the chopped prawns, red curry paste, chopped garlic and coriander to the blended salmon. Add a good pinch of salt. Get your hands in and squish the ingredients together until everything is well mixed.

Form the mixture into small one- or two-bite patties and then gently pan-fry in a little olive oil over a medium heat for about 10–12 minutes, turning frequently.

Serve with sweet chilli sauce as a dip.

Nutritional nugget

Salmon is one of the best sources of omega-3 fatty acids, which have many roles in the body, including regulating inflammation. Salmon is also an excellent source of selenium, which is essential for thyroid function and detoxification.

SERVES: 2
PREP: 10 MINS
COOK: 15 MINS

The most popular Thai dish in the UK! This is definitely one of those dishes that is amazing when done well, but done badly . . . is utterly terrible – both in taste and for your health. So many cheap versions are laden with refined sugar.

PAD THAI

125g flat rice noodles
olive oil, for stir-frying
1 large red onion, sliced
3 garlic cloves,
    finely chopped
2 spring onions,
    cut into batons
1 red chilli, chopped
    into rounds
75g shiitake mushrooms,
    sliced
juice of 1 lime
2 teaspoons Thai fish sauce
2 teaspoons soy sauce
2 teaspoons honey
2 tablespoons salted peanuts
small bunch of fresh
    coriander, torn

Put the rice noodles into a pan and cover with boiling water. Simmer for a few minutes until the noodles are cooked. Drain and set aside.

Stir-fry the onion, garlic, spring onions and chilli in a little olive oil over a medium heat for about 8 minutes until the onion has softened. Throw in the shiitake mushrooms and continue to stir-fry for another 4–5 minutes until they have softened.

Add the cooked, drained noodles and mix everything together well.

Add the lime juice, fish sauce, soy sauce and honey and mix together well to ensure everything is coated.

Sprinkle with the peanuts and the torn coriander before serving.

Green curry is one of the most delicious dishes imaginable, especially if you make the paste from scratch. This may sound a little terrifying but, trust me, it's really quite easy. Give this a whirl and I'm sure there will be no going back.

GREEN VEGETABLE CURRY

brown rice, to serve

For the paste:
2 lemongrass stalks,
　roughly chopped
2 green chillies,
　roughly chopped
4 garlic cloves,
　roughly chopped
1 large white onion,
　finely chopped
1cm piece of ginger
　or galangal root,
　peeled and chopped
4 Thai basil leaves
30g fresh coriander leaves
　and stalks
4 fresh kaffir lime leaves
½ teaspoon ground coriander
3 tablespoons Thai fish sauce
juice of 1 lime

For the curry:
coconut oil, for frying
1 large courgette, sliced
　into half circles
1 red pepper, deseeded
　and cut into chunks
1 small aubergine,
　cut into chunks
6–7 pieces of baby sweetcorn
100g shiitake mushrooms,
　sliced
2 handfuls of baby spinach
400ml can coconut milk
200ml vegetable stock

Put all the paste ingredients into a food processor and blitz to a pungent, aromatic paste.

Heat a little coconut oil in a large pan, add the curry paste and fry for around 5–8 minutes. It should turn a darker green and be less pungent in aroma.

Add the vegetables, coconut milk and stock and simmer for 10–15 minutes, or until the vegetables are tender.

Serve with brown rice.

This dish contains a brilliant variety of veggies to provide you with a whole range of vitamins, minerals and phytonutrients. Anti-inflammatory, blood sugar balancing and full of antioxidants.

Red curries are another staple Thai favourite and I absolutely adore them! I think that seafood is the perfect match for a red curry, but really you could use anything. Chicken, tofu or mixed veg will all work great too.

SERVES: 2
PREP: 15 MINS
COOK: 20 MINS

KING PRAWN RED CURRY

brown rice, to serve

For the paste:
2 teaspoons each ground
    cumin and ground
    coriander
4 red bird's-eye chillies,
    roughly chopped
1 tablespoon paprika
3 lemongrass stalks,
    roughly chopped
4cm piece of ginger or
    galangal root, peeled
    and chopped
6 fresh kaffir lime leaves
    or the finely grated zest
    of 1 lime
2 shallots, chopped
5 garlic cloves, chopped
stalks from 80g bunch
    of fresh coriander
2 tablespoons fish sauce

For the curry:
coconut oil, for frying
300g raw king prawns,
    shells removed
400ml can coconut milk
200ml fish stock
2 handfuls of baby spinach

Place the paste ingredients in a food processor and blitz into a smooth, aromatic paste.

Heat a little coconut oil in a large pan, add the curry paste and fry for around 10 minutes until it has become much darker and less pungent.

Add the coconut milk and stock and simmer for 3–4 minutes. Add the prawns and simmer for another 3–4 mintues until they are cooked. Add the spinach and allow to wilt.

Serve with brown rice.

SERVES: 2
PREP: 10 MINS
COOK: 12 MINS

I have had so many variations of this in Thailand. It's a simple dish that is perfect as a lighter option, served with some stir-fried vegetables.

MIXED SEAFOOD WITH CHILLI & LEMONGRASS

olive oil, for stir-frying
4 garlic cloves,
    finely chopped
1 large red onion, sliced
2 lemongrass stalks,
    bashed well
2 red chillies,
    roughly chopped
2cm piece of ginger,
    peeled and chopped
    into matchsticks
300g cooked mixed seafood
2 teaspoons honey
2 teaspoons Thai fish sauce
1 teaspoon corn flour
    dissolved in a little water
salt
stir-fried vegetables, to serve

Stir-fry the garlic, onion, lemongrass, chilli and ginger in a little olive oil along with a good pinch of salt for about 8 minutes until the onion is soft and the lemongrass is fragrant.

Add the mixed seafood and cook for 2–3 minutes before adding the honey and the fish sauce.

Cook for another 2–3 minutes before adding the dissolved corn flour. The sauce will thicken immediately.

Serve with stir-fried veggies.

Ohhhh, how I love chicken satay. The stuff of dreams. While most often associated with Malaysia, it is very prominent in Thailand and is on the menu of virtually every Thai takeaway in the UK.

CHICKEN SATAY

4 chicken breasts,
    sliced into thin strips
skewers (if using wooden,
    soak in cold water for
    10 minutes beforehand
    to avoid burning)
olive oil, for pan-frying

For the marinade:
120ml coconut milk
    from a 400ml can
1 tablespoon mild
    curry powder
2 teaspoons red curry paste

For the peanut sauce:
190g peanut butter
remaining coconut milk
2 tablespoons red curry paste
2 tablespoons honey
2 teaspoons soy sauce
1 large garlic clove,
    finely chopped
2–3 tablespoons water

Mix all the marinade ingredients together, ensuring everything is dissolved and well combined. Add the sliced chicken and marinate for at least 4 hours, though overnight is better.

Make the peanut sauce by adding all the ingredients together and whisking until fully combined, thick and smooth. Pour into a small saucepan and simmer for 5 minutes.

Thread 1–2 strips of chicken onto a skewer, then repeat until all the chicken is used up.

Gently pan-fry the chicken skewers in a little olive oil for 5–6 minutes each side until golden brown and fully cooked through.

Serve with the peanut dipping sauce.

Nutritional nugget

Research has shown that peanuts rival the antioxidant content of blackberries and strawberries, and are richer in antioxidants than apples, carrots or beetroot. Roasting can even increase their overall antioxidant content!

These are a gorgeous low-carb treat that make a great healthy lunch or a light evening meal. The minced lemongrass can often be found in tubes or jars in supermarkets.

STICKY CHILLI CHICKEN LETTUCE WRAPS

olive oil, for pan-frying
2 chicken breasts,
    cut into strips
1 tablespoon honey
½ teaspoon minced
    lemongrass
1 red chilli, finely chopped
1 garlic clove, finely
    chopped
½ red onion, finely
    chopped
4 cherry tomatoes,
    roughly chopped
15g fresh coriander,
    roughly chopped
8–10 small round
    lettuce leaves
salt

Pan-fry the chicken strips in a little olive oil, along with a good pinch of salt for around 8–10 minutes until fully cooked through.

Add the honey, minced lemongrass, chilli and garlic and continue to cook until the chicken gets all sticky and the sauce caramelizes. Stir continuously during this process.

Serve by placing 2–3 strips of chicken in the centre of a lettuce leaf, along with some chopped onion, tomato and coriander.

SERVES: 2
PREP: 10 MINS
COOK: 25 MINS

I adore a panang curry. In Thailand these can be utterly fabulous – intensely flavoured, rich and satisfying. This recipe had to be included.

BEEF PANANG

brown rice, to serve

For the paste:
1 red onion, finely chopped
4 garlic cloves, finely chopped
1 red chilli, halved
2 lemongrass stalks, trimmed
    and roughly chopped
1 whole star anise
1 teaspoon cumin seeds
1 teaspoon coriander seeds
½ teaspoon ground cinnamon
1 teaspoon salt
4 dry kaffir lime leaves
juice of 1 lime

For the curry:
1 tablespoon groundnut oil
400ml can coconut milk
6–8 fresh kaffir lime leaves
500g steak, finely sliced
1 tablespoon honey
2–3 tablespoons Thai fish
    sauce, to taste
juice of 1 lime
3 handfuls of baby spinach
handful of Thai basil leaves
40g roasted unsalted peanuts
1 red chilli, finely sliced

Put all the paste ingredients into a food processor and blitz into a smooth paste that doesn't have any hard pieces in it. This does take some power so if your food processor isn't powerful enough, you will have to give it some elbow grease in a pestle and mortar instead.

In a large frying pan, fry the paste in the groundnut oil for 8–10 minutes until it darkens in colour and is less pungent in aroma.

Add the coconut milk and lime leaves and simmer for 6–7 minutes until the sauce thickens.

Add the steak and continue to simmer for 5–7 minutes the steak is cooked through and the sauce is lovely and thick. Add the honey, fish sauce and lime juice.

Add the spinach and wilt down. Add the basil leaves and mix well.

Top with the peanuts and chilli slices and serve with brown rice.

SERVES: 2
PREP: 10 MINS
COOK: 15 MINS

This dish is my nod towards the many seafood-and-ginger dishes you see on Thai takeaway menus. These are generally sugar bombs and don't taste all that great. This version gives oodles of flavour and avoids all those empty calories.

KING PRAWNS WITH GINGER, COCONUT, CHILLI & LIME

olive oil, for stir-frying
1 large red onion, sliced
4 garlic cloves, finely chopped
1 red chilli, finely chopped
3cm piece of ginger, peeled
    and cut into matchsticks
165g raw king prawns,
    shells removed
2 handfuls of baby spinach
2 tablespoons desiccated
    coconut
1 teaspoon honey
2 teaspoons soy sauce
juice of 1 lime
1 teaspoon corn flour
    dissolved in a little water
1 large spring onion,
    cut into thin strips
salt
brown rice, to serve

Stir-fry the onion, garlic, chilli and ginger in a little olive oil along with a good pinch of salt for about 8 minutes until the onion has softened.

Add the king prawns and continue to stir-fry for another 2–3 minutes until the prawns are just cooked.

Add the spinach and stir until wilted.

Add the coconut, honey, soy sauce and lime juice and simmer for about a minute before adding the dissolved corn flour. The sauce will immediately thicken.

Garnish with the spring onion strips before serving with brown rice.

OK, so this one is a bit of a wild card. It's actually a fusion dish, sort of Indian dhal meets Thai curry. It really is something special and, although you won't find it on any takeaway menu, you will be so glad I included it. A perfect side dish.

THAI-STYLE LENTIL STEW

2 lemongrass stalks
olive oil, for stir-frying
1 large red onion, chopped
2 garlic cloves, chopped
1 green chilli, finely chopped
100g red lentils
200ml coconut milk
400ml vegetable stock
small bunch of fresh
    coriander, roughly chopped
1 red chilli, thinly sliced

Give the lemongrass a good wallop with a rolling pin or suitable blunt implement. This bludgeoning helps release those gorgeous oils out into the food.

Sauté the onion, garlic, bashed lemongrass and chilli in a little olive oil for about 8 minutes until the onion softens and the lemongrass is nice and fragrant.

Add the lentils and the coconut milk and simmer for 2–3 minutes.

Add the vegetable stock in small increments as though you are making a risotto, stirring continuously.

Simmer for 15–20 minutes until the lentils are soft and the texture resembles porridge. Scatter over the coriander and sliced red chilli before serving.

CHAPTER SEVEN

Grills & Classics

This chapter is for those well-known takeaway classics found on every high street. I've given them a little bit of love and tweaked them for your health!

This is not fish and chips as you know it! My version takes a little more effort, I give you that, but is so worth it from both a health and flavour perspective.

FISH, CHIPS & MUSHY PEAS

2 eggs, whisked
100g oatmeal
2 cod fillets (any white fish is OK)
olive oil
1 large sweet potato, skin left on, cut into wedges
½ white onion, finely chopped
2 garlic cloves, finely chopped
200g frozen peas
300ml vegetable stock (you won't need all of this)
salt and pepper

Nutritional nugget

Sweet potatoes are one of the best sources of beta-carotene, which is a potent antioxidant. Healthy fats can significantly increase our uptake of beta-carotene, which is where the olive oil and eggs come in!

Preheat the oven to 200°C, 180°C Fan, Gas Mark 6.

Whisk the eggs in a wide bowl and fill a similar-sized bowl with the oatmeal. Dip one of the fish fillets into the egg, turning so that it's fully covered, then dip the egg-covered fish into the oatmeal. Repeat this process so the fish has a double coating of oatmeal, then do the same with the second fillet. Place the fillets on a baking tray, brush with a little oil and bake in the oven for 20–25 minutes, until golden brown and crispy on the outside.

At the same time, put the sweet potato wedges onto a baking tray, drizzle with olive oil, add a little salt and pepper, then bake for 30 minutes, turning occasionally. They need to be golden with crisp edges and soft inside.

While the fish and wedges are cooking, sauté the onion and garlic in a little olive oil along with a good pinch of salt for about 8 minutes. Once the onion has softened, add the peas and a small amount of veg stock, and simmer until the peas are soft. Transfer this mix into a food processor and then begin to purée. You can add some more stock at this point if you want to create a thinner consistency.

Place a dollop of pea purée into the centre of each plate. Arrange a fillet of fish and some wedges on top.

This is really a nod towards the Tex-Mex food movement. There are very typical flavour profiles that accompany Tex-Mex food and this recipe is a bit of all of them in one place!

TEX-MEX BEEF BURGER

500g steak mince
1 large egg, whisked
½ red onion, finely chopped
2 large garlic cloves,
    finely chopped
3 teaspoons smoked paprika
1 teaspoon ground cumin
½ teaspoon hot chilli powder
small bunch of fresh
    coriander leaves,
    roughly chopped
2 tablespoons red
    kidney beans
olive oil, for pan-frying
salt

To serve:
multigrain rolls
baby spinach
tomato slices
mustard mayo

Put all the ingredients apart from the kidney beans into a large bowl and squidge together with your hands to ensure that everything is well combined. Season with salt. Add the kidney beans and mix in gently so as not to break them up.

Shape into 4 burger patties and pan-fry in a little olive oil for 7–8 minutes each side, turning often.

Serve in multigrain rolls with baby spinach, tomato slices and a mustard mayo.

Most takeaway chicken burgers really are awful quality and are often as dull as dishwater. Ingredients-wise, this recipe takes things back to basics and with a nice flavour kick.

CHILLI CHICKEN BURGER

250g chicken mince
25g breadcrumbs
½ red onion, finely chopped
2 garlic cloves, very finely
    chopped or minced
1 fresh red chilli, finely
    chopped, seeds kept in
1 teaspoon ground cumin
1 teaspoon ground coriander
1 teaspoon vegetable
    stock powder
small bunch of fresh
    coriander, roughly torn
juice of ½ a lime

To serve:
seeded buns
lettuce leaves
onion slices
courgette and carrot ribbons
coriander leaves

Preheat the grill to high.

Combine all of the ingredients together in a large bowl and ensure they are well mixed.

Form into 2 burger patties and place under the grill for around 15 minutes, turning halfway.

Serve in seeded buns with some crunchy fresh veg.

Veggie burgers are a big thing now. Every high-street burger joint has a veggie burger on the menu and, in all honesty, most of them are hideous. This one is super simple and tastes awesome.

VEGGIE BURGER

200g can mixed beans,
    drained and rinsed
75g wholemeal breadcrumbs
¼ large red onion,
    finely chopped
1 garlic clove, finely chopped
1½ teaspoons red curry paste
small bunch of fresh
    coriander, roughly chopped
olive oil, for brushing
salt
buns or salad, to serve

Put the beans into a large mixing bowl and mash with a fork. You are aiming for a dough/paste-like consistency but with a bit of texture.

Add the remaining ingredients and mix well. Season with salt to taste.

Form the mixture into 2 patties, brush with a little oil and place them on a foil-lined tray. Put them under the grill for about 20 minutes, turning halfway, but being careful as you do so.

These are great in a bun or with a good side salad.

This is a real little flavour bomb. Succulent, rich and full of nutrients. This is definitely indulgent health.

JALAPEÑO BURGER WITH GUACAMOLE

seeded buns, to serve
   (optional)

For the burgers:
500g steak mince
1 large egg, whisked
½ red onion, finely chopped
2 large garlic cloves,
   finely chopped
2 tablespoons pickled
   jalapeños
salt and pepper

For the guacamole:
1 very ripe avocado
½ red onion, finely chopped
2 garlic cloves, finely chopped
1 green chilli, finely chopped
juice of 1 lime
small bunch of fresh
   coriander, roughly chopped

Mix all the burger ingredients together and season well. Form into 4 patties and pan-fry for 7–8 minutes each side.

To make the guacamole, scoop the avocado flesh into a bowl. Add the remaining ingredients and mash together. Season well.

Regardless of whether you have the burger with or without a bun, make sure that it's served with a generous dollop of guacamole on top!

Nutritional nugget

There are few vitamins and minerals NOT found in avocados! They can also help support healthy blood sugar balance and are great for feeling satisfied after a meal.

Believe it or not, sandwiches are one of Britain's top takeaways! This is mostly a lunchtime phenomenon, with the well-known delivery companies reporting that sandwiches are still the most requested item. The BLT is up there on the popular list and, let's be fair, most of the time it is a soggy mess. Time to give it an upgrade.

BANGING BLT

4 rashers nitrate-free bacon
1 teaspoon mild curry powder
1 tablespoon mayonnaise
2 slices multigrain/
    granary bread
a few red lettuce leaves
7–8 baby spinach leaves
½ beef tomato, sliced
¼ avocado, sliced

Cook the bacon under the grill until it's crisp along the edges.

Mix the curry powder into the mayonnaise.

Place the leaves on one of the slices of bread first, then the tomato, then the avocado, then the bacon, then dollop over the curry mayo. Top with the other slice of bread. Banging!

These really can be the good, the bad and the ugly. There's no reason at all why they should be swimming in glucose syrup, dyed a fluorescent red or mummified with MSG. A few simple, natural ingredients and these can turn out absolutely stunning – and keep the nasties at bay!

HOT WINGS

8 chicken wings

For the marinade:
1 tablespoon honey
1 teaspoon rice vinegar
1 teaspoon smoked paprika
1 teaspoon medium to hot
   chilli powder (according
   to how brave you are)
½ teaspoon garlic powder

Preheat the oven to 180°C, 160°C Fan, Gas Mark 4.

Put the chicken wings in a sandwich or freezer bag.

Mix all of the marinade ingredients together and pour into the bag. If you have time, leave to marinate in the fridge for a couple of hours, or even overnight.

Shake the bag well to ensure the chicken is completely coated. Empty the bag contents onto a baking tray, ensuring any leftover marinade is poured over the chicken.

Bake for 25–30 minutes, checking halfway through and turning.

OK – it's a leap, I know, but recreating that crispy Southern Fried Chicken vibe at home isn't that difficult, and you can get creative with the flavour profiles too.

KOULD-BE FRIED CHICKEN

75ml milk
2 chicken breasts,
    cut into strips
25g panko breadcrumbs
1 tablespoon self-raising flour
1 teaspoon smoked paprika
1 teaspoon garlic powder
½ teaspoon mustard powder
½ teaspoon dried thyme
½ teaspoon dried oregano

Pour the milk into a bowl and add the chicken to it, turning it a few times. Keep the bowl of milk and chicken in the fridge for at least 2 hours, ideally overnight.

Preheat the oven to 180°C, 160°C Fan, Gas Mark 4.

Place the panko breadcrumbs, flour, spices and herbs all together in a sandwich bag and mix together well.

Remove the chicken strips from the milk and add them straight to the bag. Shake well until the chicken is coated. Remove the strips one by one and lay them on a baking tray.

Bake for 25–30 minutes until the crumb coating is a golden brown.

This is another popular item at the well-known sub sandwich shops. Many people shy away from red meat and there certainly is a connection between excess red meat and the risk of many diseases, including cardiovascular disease and colorectal cancers. That being said, the poison is in the dose and there are certainly benefits to be had if eaten once in a while.

SERVES: 1
PREP: 10 MINS
COOK: 5–10 MINS

THE STEAK SARNIE

1 small steak, fat trimmed
1 wholemeal sub roll or bap
1 handful of baby kale
1 tablespoon grated
  red cabbage
1 tablespoon grated carrot
1 tablespoon mayonnaise
2–3 slices red onion, separated
1 tablespoon grated Cheddar
1 teaspoon English mustard

Cook the steak to your liking. Slice it into strips.

Add the kale leaves to the bottom of the roll. Mix the grated carrot and red cabbage together with the mayo to make a slaw. Add on top of the kale. Add the sliced steak. Top with the onion slices and then the cheese. Spread the mustard on the upper inside surface of the roll.

Nutritional nugget

Beef can help support energy levels due to its B12 and iron content, both of which are needed for the production of haemoglobin, the oxygen-carrying pigment in our red blood cells.

Typically when you go to any of the grill outlets and order a portion of ribs, you are basically ordering a pint of sugar! You can achieve that same sticky vibe, plus oodles of flavour, by swapping the vast amounts of sugar syrup for a little honey. Some sugar, yes, but a lot less and with a few minerals to boot.

SERVES: 2
PREP: 10 MINS
COOK: 2¼–2½ HOURS

ROASTED RIBS

3 teaspoons Chinese
    five-spice powder
1 teaspoon garlic powder
    or garlic salt
sprinkle of cracked
    black pepper
1 rack of pork ribs
1 tablespoon honey
1 tablespoon water
1 teaspoon sesame oil
2 spring onions, sliced
rice or potatoes and
    green salad, to serve

Preheat the oven to 150°C, 130°C Fan, Gas Mark 2.

Mix the five-spice powder, garlic powder and pepper together. Lay the ribs on a board or tray. Sprinkle half of the five-spice mixture over one side and rub it all over. Turn the rack and repeat on the other side.

Line a deep baking tray with foil and place the seasoned ribs onto it. Roast for 1½ hours.

Turn the oven to 180°C, 160°C Fan, Gas Mark 4.

Mix the honey, water and sesame oil together and whisk well with a fork to make an emulsion.

Remove the ribs from the oven, pour the honey liquid over them and return to the oven for 45 minutes–1 hour.

Scatter over the sliced spring onions.

Serve with rice or potatoes and a large green salad.

Family Feasts

This chapter will help you knock up a delicious fakeaway feast with minimal fuss. Cheaper, tastier and healthier than your usual takeaway . . . perfect for when you have the whole family round on a Friday-night. Get the kids involved and it will be fun too!

This Indian feast is incredibly easy – and cheap – to create. Chana masala freezes well, so it's a perfect dish to make in advance. Many of the ingredients in these recipes you will already have at home, meaning your shopping list will be kept to a minimum – both in items and price.

Indian Feast

PALAK PANEER
TANDOORI CHICKEN
SAAG ALOO
CHANA MASALA

SHOPPING LIST

FRESH
3 large onion
17 garlic cloves
1 fresh hot chilli
15cm piece of ginger
750g potatoes
1kg fresh spinach
100g baby spinach
¼ of a lemon
1 green chilli, chopped
1 medium tomato,
    finely chopped
250g paneer (tofu can be
    used as an alternative)
150ml Greek yogurt
8 chicken thighs,
    on the bone

STORE CUPBOARD
3 teaspoons turmeric
1½ teaspoons chilli powder
½ teaspoon cumin seeds
1 teaspoon ground cumin
1½ teaspoon garam masala
2 tablespoons coconut cream
400g can chopped tomatoes
1 tablespoon tahini
400g can chickpeas, drained

PALAK PANEER (P.24)

TANDOORI CHICKEN (P.27)

SAAG ALOO (P.18)

CHANA MASALA (P.28)

Prep the spring rolls and the peanut dipping sauce in advance – even the day before – and simply place the spring rolls in the oven while everything else is cooking. Both the sweet and sour chicken and king prawns are one-pot dishes and super simple to make. You'll have a Chinese feast in no time!

Chinese Feast

EGG & VEGETABLE FRIED RICE
SWEET & SOUR CHICKEN
KING PRAWNS WITH GINGER & SPRING ONIONS
BAKED SPRING ROLLS

SHOPPING LIST

FRESH
9 garlic cloves, finely chopped
2½ red onion, finely chopped
8 spring onions, finely chopped
4 tablespoons frozen peas
2 large eggs
2 red pepper, deseeded
   and cut into 2cm chunks
1 green pepper, deseeded
   and cut into 2cm chunks
2 chicken breasts, sliced
2 tablespoons pineapple juice
10cm piece of ginger, peeled
   and cut into thin slices
170g raw king prawns
½ courgette, cut into batons
1 large carrot, cut into thin strips
a wedge of red cabbage, shredded
2 small spring onions, white part
   finely sliced, green part cut
   lengthwise into thin strips
1 red chilli, finely chopped

STORE CUPBOARD
4 tablespoons honey
1 tablespoon passata
3 teaspoons cider vinegar
120g brown rice
8 teaspoons soy sauce
1 tablespoon smooth
   peanut butter
2½ teaspoon Chinese
   five-spice powder
12 spring roll wrappers
½ tablespoon toasted sesame oil
   (or replace with vegetable oil)
2 teaspoons oyster sauce
dash of rice wine vinegar
1 teaspoon corn flour dissolved
   in 1 tablespoon water

EGG & VEGETABLE FRIED RICE (P.38)

SWEET & SOUR CHICKEN (P.46)

KING PRAWNS WITH GINGER
& SPRING ONIONS (P.51)

BAKED SPRING ROLLS (P.57)

Prep the pizza in advance and set aside while you get on with the rest of the feast – and make sure you get the kids involved! It can go in the oven at the same time as the parmigiana. The sauce for the spag bol freezes beautifully so having some pre-made will mean everything is that little bit easier. We have spaghetti two ways here, so there's something for everyone. All you need is a huge green salad and you'll have a cracking Italian feast.

Italian Feast

PIZZA WITH A PUNCH
SPAGHETTI BOLOGNESE
AUBERGINE PARMIGIANA
SPAGHETTI PUTTANESCA

SHOPPING LIST

FRESH
3½ large red onion
9 garlic cloves
1 red pepper
500g lean minced beef
2 large aubergines
100g ricotta
100g Parmesan
200g mozzarella
10 anchovy fillets
1 fresh green chilli
2–3 tablespoons chopped
   fresh parsley
3 handfuls of baby spinach
75g blue cheese
4 teaspoons pesto

To serve
salad ingredients

STORE CUPBOARD
180g dry red lentils
500g pack of ready-mixed
   multigrain/seeded
   wholemeal bread mix
500g wholemeal spaghetti
8 tablespoons tomato passata
500g wholemeal spaghetti
5 x 400g cans chopped tomatoes
2 teaspoons dried oregano
150g (drained weight)
   pitted black olives
2 tablespoons small capers
125ml red wine
olive oil
salt and pepper

PIZZA WITH A PUNCH (P.72)

SPAGHETTI BOLOGNESE (P.63)

AUBERGINE PARMIGIANA (P.66)

SPAGHETTI PUTTANESCA (P.69)

Sushi rolls can be made in advance and kept in the fridge, so you can get on with the rest of your Japanese feast. The chicken yakitori skewers can also be done in advance – just pop them in a frying pan for the final 10 minutes of cooking.

Japanese Feast

....

BEGINNERS' SUSHI ROLLS
VEGAN DONBURI
YAKI SOBA
CHICKEN YAKITORI

....

SHOPPING LIST

FRESH

1 large red onion
4 garlic cloves
2cm piece of ginger
2 large spring onions
6–7 shiitake mushrooms
165g king prawns
3 handfuls of baby spinach
200g boneless skinless
    chicken thighs
1 red pepper
150g shiitake mushrooms
2 handfuls of shredded greens
1 large spring onion
½ cucumber
1 avocado
225g smoked salmon,
    crab meat or tuna

STORE CUPBOARD

120g soba noodles
2 tablespoons pickled ginger
1 teaspoon corn flour
150g uncooked short-grain rice
120g brown rice
3 tablespoons rice vinegar
4 nori seaweed sheets
3 tablespoons mirin
    (Japanese rice vinegar)
3 tablespoons soy sauce
1 tablespoon agave nectar
    (or honey)
2 tablespoons Worcestershire sauce
65ml soy sauce
2 tablespoons oyster sauce
2 tablespoons honey
50ml mirin (Japanese rice vinegar)
30ml sake
salt
bamboo skewers

BEGINNERS' SUSHI ROLLS (P.100)

VEGAN DONBURI (P.97)

YAKI SOBA (P.89)

CHICKEN YAKITORI (P.90)

Middle Eastern food is made for a feast! All of these recipes are so simple to make, and the falafel can even be prepared well in advance and frozen until you need them.

Middle Eastern Feast

HUMMUS BOWLS & BABAGANOUSH
FALAFEL WITH TAHINI DRESSING
CHICKEN SHISH PITTA
VEGGIE PLATTER

SHOPPING LIST

FRESH

9½ garlic cloves, crushed
½ small bunch fresh
    flatleaf parsley
1¼ red onion
2 free-range eggs
4½ lemons
4 large aubergines
2 teaspoons pomegranate seeds
2 handfuls of parsley
½ a head of cauliflower
200g ripe tomatoes
½ large cucumber
50g radishes
1 spring onion
small bunch of fresh mint
2 wholemeal pitta bread (1 stale)
2 tablespoons plain yogurt
1 skinless chicken breast
2 tablespoons goat's cheese
small handful of baby spinach
red onion, finely sliced

STORE CUPBOARD

4 x 400g tins chickpeas
3½ teaspoons cumin
1 teaspoon cinnamon
1 teaspoon smoked paprika
9 tablespoons tahini
2 teaspoons cider vinegar
1½ teaspoons ground coriander
½ teaspoon sumac
1 teaspoon sesame seeds
a drizzle of sesame oil
2 tablespoons wholemeal flour
olive oil
salt and pepper

HUMMUS BOWLS & BABAGANOUSH (P.109 & P.110)

FALAFEL WITH TAHINI DRESSING (P.104)

CHICKEN SHISH PITTA (P.112)

VEGGIE PLATTER (P.120)

Prepare for this feast by making the paste for the green curry in advance. It will keep in the fridge for three days, so you can be well ahead of the game! Prep the chicken satay the day before and leave to marinate in the fridge overnight. You could make the satay sauce the day before too, then all you need to do is pan-fry for 10 minutes before tucking in.

Thai Feast

GREEN VEGETABLE CURRY
CHICKEN SATAY
PAD THAI
KING PRAWNS WITH GINGER, COCONUT & LIME

SHOPPING LIST

FRESH

1 large white onion
2 large red onion
12 garlic cloves
3 spring onions
2 red chilli
2 green chillies
75g shiitake mushrooms
3 limes
small bunch of fresh coriander
2 lemongrass stalks
4cm piece of ginger
1 large courgette
1 red pepper
1 small aubergine
6–7 pieces of baby sweetcorn
100g shiitake mushrooms
4 handfuls of baby spinach
4 chicken breasts
165g raw king prawns

STORE CUPBOARD

125g flat rice noodles
2 teaspoons Thai fish sauce
6 teaspoons soy sauce
3 tablespoons honey
2 tablespoons salted peanuts
1 teaspoon corn flour dissolved
   in a little water
2 tablespoons desiccated coconut
2 tablespoons red curry paste
190g peanut butter
4 fresh kaffir lime leaves
½ teaspoon ground
   coriander powder
3 tablespoons Thai fish sauce
4 Thai basil leaves
1 x 400ml can coconut milk
200ml vegetable stock
1 tablespoon mild curry powder
2 teaspoons red curry paste
wooden skewers

GREEN VEGETABLE CURRY (P.128)

CHICKEN SATAY (P.134)

PAD THAI (P.126)

**KING PRAWNS WITH GINGER,
COCONUT & LIME (P.140)**

Grills & Classics Feast

ROASTED RIBS
HOT WINGS
JALAPEÑO BURGER WITH GUACAMOLE
VEGGIE BURGER

SHOPPING LIST

FRESH
1 rack of pork ribs
8 chicken wings
500g steak mince
1 large egg
2 spring onions
½ red onion
5 garlic cloves
1 very ripe avocado
1 green chilli
juice of 1 lime
small bunch of fresh coriander
small bunch of fresh coriander

To serve
burger buns
salad
rice/potatoes

STORE CUPBOARD
75g wholemeal breadcrumbs
200g can mixed beans
2 tablespoons pickled jalapeños
1½ teaspoons red curry paste
2 tablespoon honey
1 teaspoon rice vinegar
1 teaspoon smoked paprika
1 teaspoon medium to hot
  chilli powder
½ teaspoon garlic powder
1 teaspoon sesame oil
olive oil

ROASTED RIBS (P.165)

HOT WINGS (P.159)

JALAPEÑO BURGER WITH GUACAMOLE (P.154)

VEGGIE BURGER (P.153)

INDEX

LIST OF RECIPES BY FOOD GROUP

MEAT

Chicken
Top Marks Tikka Masala (p.12)
Chicken Rogan Josh (p.18)
Tandoori Chicken (p.22)
Sweet and Sour Chicken (p.36)
Kung Pao Chicken (p.50)
Chicken Koftas (p.80)
Chicken Shish Pitta with Goat's
    Cheese Yogurt Dressing (p.86)
Chicken Katsu Curry (p.98)
Miso Ramen (p.102)
Chicken Yakitori (p.106)
Chicken Satay (p.130)
Sticky Chilli Chicken Lettuce
    Wraps (p.132)
Hot Wings (p.152)
Kould-be Fried Chicken (p.154)
Chilli Chicken Burger (p.160)

Duck
Roasted Duck Breast with Garlic
    and Ginger Greens (p.44)

Pork
Tagliatelle Carbonarish (p.74)
Banging BLT (p.150)
Roasted Ribs (p.158)

Beef
Beef & Broccoli in Black Bean Sauce (p.48)
Low-carb Lasagne (p.56)
Spaghetti Bolognese (p.60)
Fasulia (p.90)
Beef Panang (p.136)
Tex-mex Beef Burger (p.144)
Jalapeno Burger with Guacamole (p.148)
The Steak Sarnie (p.156)

FISH
King Prawns with Cashew
    Nuts (p.40)
King Prawns with Ginger
    & Spring Onions (p.46)
Spaghetti Puttanesca (p.64)
Seafood Linguine (p.72)
Chilli Squid (p.100)
Yaki Soba (p.104)
Cod with Miso Sauce &
    Gingered Greens (p.108)
Curry Udon (p.114)
Beginners' Sushi Rolls (p.116)
Salmon & Prawn Cakes (p.120)
Pad Thai (p.122) *contains fish
    sauce so not veggie
Green Vegetable Curry (p.124)
    *contains fish sauce so
    not veggie
King Prawn Red Curry (p.126)
Mixed Seafood with Chilli
    & Lemongrass (p.128)
King Prawns with Ginger,
    Coconut, Chilli & Lime (p.138)
Fish Chips & Mushy Peas (p.142)

VEGGIE
Saag Aloo (ve) (p.14)
Tarka Dhal (ve) (p.16.)
Palak Paneer (p.20)
Chana Masala (ve) (p.24)
Vegetable Dansak (ve) (p.26)
Bombay Potatoes (ve) (p.28)
Power Pilau (ve) (p.30)
Egg & Vegetable Fried Rice (p.34)
Vegetable Chow Mein (p.38)
Ma Po Tofu (p.42)
Baked Spring Rolls (ve)(p.52)

Aubergine Parmigiana (p.58)
  *though NB only veggie if using
  an alternative to Parmesan
Penne Arrabbiata (p.62)
Sweet Potato Gnocchi with Walnut
  & Goat's Cheese Pesto (p.66)
  *NB only veggie if using
  veggie rennet
Pizza with a Punch (p.68)
  *NB only veggie if using
  veggie rennet
Slow-burn Risotto (p.71)
Falafel with Tahini Dressing (p.78)
Hummus Bowls (p.82)
Baba Ganoush (p.84)
Mujadarra (p.88)
Libyan Shakshuka (p.92)
Veggie Platter (p.94)
Okonomiyaki (p.110)
Vegan Donburi (ve) (p.112)
Thai-style Lentil Stew (ve) (p.134)
Veggie Burger (p.146)

USEFUL STORECUPBOARD INGREDIENTS

Brown rice
Canned chickpeas
Canned tomatoes
Chilli flakes
Chilli powder
Chinese five spice powder
Cider vinegar
Coconut cream
Coconut milk
Corn flour
Cumin seeds
Dried green lentils

Dried oregano
Dried red lentils
Dried thyme
Olive oil
Flat rice noodles
Smoked paprika
Garam masala
Ground cinnamon
Ground coriander
Ground cumin
Honey
Mirin
Miso paste
Oyster sauce
Panko breadcrumbs
Passata
Plain flour
Red wine vinegar
Rice wine vinegar
Sesame oil
Shortgrain rice
Soba noodles
Soy sauce
Tahini
Thai fish sauce
Turmeric
Udon noodles
Vegetable stock
Wholemeal spaghetti